Joy Runs Deeper

D1036397

Joy Runs Deeper
Bronia and Joseph Beker

JOSEPH BEKER'S MEMOIR TRANSLATED
FROM YIDDISH BY VIVIAN FELSEN

THE AZRIELI FOUNDATION
www.azrielifoundation.org

Cover and book design by Mark Goldstein
Endpaper maps by Martin Gilbert
Map on page xxix by François Blanc

LIBRARY AND ARCHIVES CANADA CATALOGUING IN PUBLICATION

Beker, Bronia, 1920–, author
     Joy runs deeper / Bronia and Joseph Beker; Joseph
Beker's memoir translated from Yiddish by Vivian Felsen.

(The Azrieli series of Holocaust survivor memoirs. VI)
Includes bibliographical references and index.
ISBN 978-1-897470-45-9 (pbk.)

1. Beker, Bronia, 1920–. 2. Beker, Joseph, 1913–1988. 3. Holocaust, Jewish (1939–1945) – Poland – Personal narratives. 4. Jews – Poland – Biography. 5. Holocaust survivors – Canada – Biography. I. Beker, Joseph, 1913–1988, author II. Azrieli Foundation, issuing body III. Title. IV. Series: Azrieli series of Holocaust survivor memoirs. Series VI

DS134.72.B45A3 2014   940.53'18092   C2014-906154-4

MIX
Paper from responsible sources
FSC
www.fsc.org   FSC® C004191

PRINTED IN CANADA

The Azrieli Series of Holocaust Survivor Memoirs

Naomi Azrieli, Publisher

Jody Spiegel, Program Director
Arielle Berger, Managing Editor
Elizabeth Lasserre, Senior Editor, French-Language Editions
Aurélien Bonin, French-Language Educational Outreach and Events
Catherine Person, Quebec Educational Outreach and Events
Elin Beaumont, English-Language Educational Outreach and Events
Tim MacKay, New Media and Marketing

Susan Roitman, Executive Assistant and Office Manager (Toronto)
Mary Mellas, Executive Assistant and Human Resources (Montreal)
Eric Bélisle, Administrative Assistant

Mark Goldstein, Art Director
François Blanc, Cartographer
Bruno Paradis, Layout, French-Language Editions

Contents

Series Preface:
In their own words. . .

In telling these stories, the writers have liberated themselves. For so many years we did not speak about it, even when we became free people living in a free society. Now, when at last we are writing about what happened to us in this dark period of history, knowing that our stories will be read and live on, it is possible for us to feel truly free. These unique historical documents put a face on what was lost, and allow readers to grasp the enormity of what happened to six million Jews – one story at a time.

David J. Azrieli, C.M., C.Q., M.Arch
Holocaust survivor and founder, The Azrieli Foundation

Since the end of World War II, over 30,000 Jewish Holocaust survivors have immigrated to Canada. Who they are, where they came from, what they experienced and how they built new lives for themselves and their families are important parts of our Canadian heritage. The Azrieli Foundation's Holocaust Survivor Memoirs Program was established to preserve and share the memoirs written by those who survived the twentieth-century Nazi genocide of the Jews of Europe and later made their way to Canada. The program is guided by the conviction that each survivor of the Holocaust has a remarkable story to tell, and that such stories play an important role in education about tolerance and diversity.

Millions of individual stories are lost to us forever. By preserving the stories written by survivors and making them widely available to a broad audience, the Azrieli Foundation's Holocaust Survivor Memoirs Program seeks to sustain the memory of all those who perished at the hands of hatred, abetted by indifference and apathy. The personal accounts of those who survived against all odds are as different as the people who wrote them, but all demonstrate the courage, strength, wit and luck that it took to prevail and survive in such terrible adversity. The memoirs are also moving tributes to people – strangers and friends – who risked their lives to help others, and who, through acts of kindness and decency in the darkest of moments, frequently helped the persecuted maintain faith in humanity and courage to endure. These accounts offer inspiration to all, as does the survivors' desire to share their experiences so that new generations can learn from them.

The Holocaust Survivor Memoirs Program collects, archives and publishes these distinctive records and the print editions are available free of charge to libraries, educational institutions and Holocaust-education programs across Canada. They are also available for sale to the general public at bookstores. All revenues to the Azrieli Foundation from the sales of the Azrieli Series of Holocaust Survivor Memoirs go toward the publishing and educational work of the memoirs program.

The Azrieli Foundation would like to express appreciation to the following people for their invaluable efforts in producing this book: Sherry Dodson (Maracle Press), Sir Martin Gilbert, Barbara Kamieński, Farla Klaiman, Therese Parent, Mia Spiro, and Margie Wolfe and Emma Rodgers of Second Story Press.

About the Glossary

The following memoir contains a number of terms, concepts and historical references that may be unfamiliar to the reader. For information on major organizations; significant historical events and people; geographical locations; religious and cultural terms; and foreign-language words and expressions that will help give context and background to the events described in the text, please see the glossary beginning on page 81.

Introduction

Children of survivors are left with legacies as powerfully daunting as they are inspiring. Although our parents' youth was shattered by unspeakable pain and profound loss, they still managed to determinedly pick up the broken pieces and stoically re-build their lives. Their tales of toughness and tenacity light our paths and teach us the kind of heroic fearlessness it takes to survive. Lessons learned from our parents inspire and challenge us to work hard, be successful and live out not just our dreams, but their unrealized ones as well. Their heroism drives us relentlessly.

Unlike some survivors who were reluctant to talk or kept their stories secret, my parents were adamant about recounting every detail of their war experience, time and time again. I remember, as a child, hiding under the bed just because I didn't want to hear any more of their "war stories." Now, I realize it was precisely their storytelling that made me who I am, colouring my personal philosophies, imparting resiliency and instilling in me a precious instinct for survival.

"Don't be afraid and never give up." That was my father's famous motto, the mindset that saw him through the war. My mother's modus operandi, which could chip away any potential optimism, was more pragmatic: "Expect the worst and you won't be disappointed." It certainly wasn't an upbeat way of viewing the world, but it stemmed from her motherly attempt to protect us and spare us pain. While our mother's world view certainly affected us, even to this day, it was our father's edict that we really took to heart, an order that still carries my sister and me through all our trials.

After surviving the war, my parents spent three years in a Displaced Persons camp in Austria before boarding a boat to Halifax. My mother's uncle Isaac Gold, who'd immigrated to Canada well before the war, sponsored them and in 1948, they embarked on their new adventure with a beautiful little girl – my sister Marilyn – and untold optimism. They were penniless, but determined to make a new life for themselves. While in Austria, my mother had been trained as a cosmetician through the Organization for Rehabilitation through Training (ORT). My father, quite the jack-of-all-trades, had brazenly raised his hand when he heard they were looking for furriers in Canada. Though my father had no training whatsoever in that field, he was conveniently suffering from a bout of eczema when the prospective furriers were being tested at a sewing machine, and due to his bandaged arms, he couldn't take the test. So he was just waved through, and luckily made the list to head to Canada.

When my parents eventually arrived in Toronto in 1948, they moved in with my mother's uncle and his ailing wife, and secured jobs: My dad first worked at a paper box factory and then at a slipper factory. My mom, unable to score a job as a cosmetician because she didn't speak English, got hired at a pants factory for $12 a week. They scrimped and saved and four years later, in 1952, the year I was born, they managed to put a down payment on a three-storey house in a family-oriented neighbourhood in Toronto's west end. My parents, my sister and I occupied the main floor of the house, while a colourful and constantly changing assortment of "roomers" inhabited the other two floors. We never could have afforded to live in that wonderful old place if it hadn't been for that cast of tenants helping to subsidize our mortgage payments, but they provided much more than that for our family – sharing our home with that eclectic array of characters gave us a sense of extended family and a feeling of camaraderie. My mother's greatest joy was the delicious feeling of a household that was *leibidich* – the Yiddish word for lively. And my generous dad delighted in socializing with the assorted international personalities, "interviewing" them at the kitchen table, sometimes over shot glasses of Crown Royal whiskey, imparting his wisdom and learning from his tenants.

Always adamant about wanting to be his own boss, my ambitious father, along with two of his colleagues at the slipper factory, decided to make a bold move and start their own slipper manufacturing enterprise in the basement of our house. They called their fledgling company Quality Slippers, and they specialized in children's and women's novelty plush slippers. As the orders grew, they eventually got a proper shop downtown, in a decrepit space in the heart of the *schmatte* (garment) district. My dad went to work at the shop seven days a week, and on weekdays he'd be gone from seven in the morning until seven at night. He enjoyed calling the shots in his business, and was loved and respected by all the terrific people who worked for him, mainly Italian immigrants. But aside from the glories of making deals, he had little respect for the nature of his business and always reminded my sister and me that he'd never be working in a slipper factory if he'd been born in Canada and enjoyed the opportunities available to the native born. I'll never forget the sweat on his brow as he toiled in that sweltering factory in the heat of summer, often sitting at those little machines himself, expertly sewing soles on slippers. I remember feeling sorry that he had to work so hard in order to give the four of us a good life, but I adored him for it and knew that he loved us all deeply and unconditionally.

My mom stopped working when I was born and became a full-time housewife. She was the consummate ultra-feminine, dedicated wife, totally devoted to my father. Because he'd rescued her during the war, she felt indebted to him. He was her hero and she'd do anything to please him. While both my parents were honest by nature, my mother often felt that she was honest to a fault. She always spoke her mind and sometimes thought she got into trouble because of it. She was such a highly emotional person that wearing her heart on her sleeve came naturally, and she instilled in me the belief that as long as you told the truth, nothing could ever hurt you. She deeply believed that all we have is ourselves and that it was imperative to accept that. My mother was fairly well read – an intellectual by nature – and felt strongly about the value of exposing us to the arts. Regular trips to the public library were always a treat for my sister and me. She took me to ballet lessons when I was four and then piano lessons at seven. Art and drama lessons followed in later years.

While Shabbat dinners every Friday night were de rigueur at our house, I wasn't aware of how adamant my parents were about making sure I had a good "Jewish" upbringing until it was time for Grade 1. They enrolled me for full-time studies at Talmud Torah, the Associated Hebrew Day School, where half my day would be spent learning Hebrew. My sister had gone to after-school Hebrew lessons for a brief period, but now that my parents were doing a little better financially, they felt a full-time private Jewish school would be ideal for me.

Around this time, we became even more conscious of our Jewish identity because we moved from the old downtown neighbourhood, mostly inhabited by Italian families, to a modern bungalow in a newly developed suburban neighbourhood that had a predominantly Jewish population. My parents promptly joined the Orthodox synagogue around the corner, even though they were really Conservative. And thanks to the nice Orthodox family living next door, I was exposed to myriad traditional practices, from Saturday evening *havdalah* ceremonies to mark the end of Shabbat, to erecting a Sukkah, small hut, for the autumn holiday of Sukkot. I often wondered why my parents wanted to be part of such an Orthodox community. After all, they could have joined the neighbouring Conservative shul just a little further from the house. I realize now that this was likely an attempt to get back to their roots, to hear the prayers recited in the same way as when they were growing up, harkening back to that innocent time before the war, when life was so simple and their sense of religion and shared community so strong.

My mother had a wonderfully high energy level, and though she may have misspent some of that energy worrying – she used to call herself a "professional worrier" – she also got involved in a wide assortment of projects, some quite creative. Beside being a master of crocheting and completing numerous needlepoint tapestries, she was given a sewing machine from my dad, and all through the 1960s she made my sister and me some of the most fabulous clothes imaginable, usually inspired by the pages of her beloved *Vogue* and *Harper's Bazaar*. She signed up for conversational Hebrew lessons, was an ardent volunteer for Meals on Wheels and one of the hospitals, and for decades was a passionate member of the Hadassah organization. She took dozens of driving lessons before successfully getting her driver's licence, eventually learned how to swim, sang in a choir and even signed up for French lessons for a brief period. She prided herself on her baking skills, excelling at cinnamon rolls, banana bread and apple cake. Her *Mohnkuchen*, or poppy seed rolls, lemon meringue pie and flourless nut cake were mouth-watering and memorable.

Family trips were a great source of joy to my parents, and we tried to take them as often as possible. Our first foreign excursions, which began around 1957, were car rides to New York in my dad's second-hand, pale green, 1953 Buick. With Motor League "Trip-Tiks" in hand, and my mom acting as chief navigator, my dad drove the four of us to the exotic wilds of Coney Island, where we stayed with my mom's half-brother Harry and his wife, Dora. My mother had two other half-siblings in Brooklyn, Lena and Rose, who'd also immigrated to the United States before the war. It was marvellous to spend time with them and their families, and it gave us the feeling that the four of us weren't so alone in the world after all.

Shortly thereafter, we began to take regular drives to Passaic, New Jersey to visit my father's American-born cousins, who also gave us a joyful sense of belonging. They encouraged us to explore the wonders of Miami Beach, and in the early 1960s, having traded up to a used 1959 Chrysler, we took on the challenge of extended annual motor trips to the Sunshine State over the Christmas holidays. Those chaotic drives, rife with my sister and I fighting in the backseat and my parents arguing over directions in the front, were my idea of a great time. I especially savoured the overnight motel stops at Howard Johnson's, complete with vibrating beds and stacks of pancakes for breakfast.

My parents' devotion to our tiny family was equalled by their dedication to their fantastic group of friends, all Polish Holocaust survivors, some of whom they met in the Austrian DP camp, and some once they arrived in Toronto. One dear group of these friends, who called themselves "The Reading Club," had weekly gatherings at each other's houses where they read Yiddish books aloud. Often at my parents' dinner parties, the guests would break out in song, swept up by joyful memories of pre-war times before all the loss and terror, when everyone was filled with hope and life was sweet.

As the years went by, my parents did a bit of travelling together, enjoying summers with their friends in Georgian Bay, as well as trips to Mexico, Rome, Athens, Los Angeles (to visit my sister, when she eventually moved there) and, of course, their beloved Israel, where my mom adored visiting her relatives. But their vacations were limited, and they seemed to be saving for the day when my dad would retire, so they could really go off and enjoy themselves. It was sad to watch my dad work so hard, to scrimp and save all his life, only to become ill around retirement age. In and out of hospitals for several years with a worsening heart condition, he was eventually forced to give up his little business in 1984, and then spent a good chunk of his savings trying to get help at a prestigious Boston hospital, after doctors in Toronto had given up on him. Four years later, in 1988, nine months after seeing his first grandchild born, my dad passed away. I was glad that at least he'd lived to see my daughter.

My mom felt completely lost without my dad by her side but she soldiered on, continuing to throw herself into her hobbies and volunteer work and savouring spending time with her beautiful granddaughters Bekky and Joey, my second daughter, born the year after my dad died, and named after him. In 1995, I had the thrill of taking my mother back to her native Poland, to celebrate the launch of Fashion Television on Polish TV. She was so excited to be able to go back to a place where she could speak the language fluently. But as keen as she was to try and re-visit her hometown of Kozowa, it had now become part of Ukraine, and I discouraged her from going back to this potentially painful place. Still, she experienced true elation in being able to return to Poland, this time as a celebrated "v IP," after having left there so ravaged and abused. She acted as our translator and even had the chance to address the press conference for the launch, held in a former Warsaw palace. Everybody was so charmed and impressed by her that part of the little speech she'd prepared in Polish even made the news on TV that evening. It may have been her proudest moment.

Now, at age ninety-three and suffering from Parkinson's, my mom has slowed down considerably, but she still has a gorgeous twinkle in her eye. She still takes enormous pride in her two granddaughters and my sister and me, and continues to be wonderfully stylish. She was my first true style icon and she inspires me in countless ways. Ultimately, both my parents taught us the meaning of courage and dignity and the necessity of forging ahead no matter what.

My mother wrote her powerful memoir more than thirty years ago, always dreaming that my sister, a documentary filmmaker and screenwriting professor, might turn her story into a movie. While that hasn't happened yet, my daughter Bekky did write a play based on my mother's memoir, which was given a reading by Toronto's Harold Green Jewish Theatre a few years ago. It wasn't until rather recently that I learned that my dad had also begun writing his memoirs, longhand, in Yiddish, shortly before he died. His story, unfortunately left incomplete, was only translated for the first time this past year. My sister and I had never read it before and we were moved to see all the wit and daring in some of the remarkable stories he told so well. But beyond all the inspiration and lessons to be learned from the extraordinary lives of both our parents, it's their charming recollections of shtetl life, painting vivid pictures of a spirited time gone by, that I'm certain will enthrall you and that are destined to leave a legacy for generations to come.

Jeanne Beker
Toronto, 2014

Foreword

Bronia and Josio (Joseph) Beker's *Joy Runs Deeper* offers rich insight into a vanished Jewish civilization. Their memoirs begin in the pre-Holocaust shtetl of Kozowa (Galicia/Ukraine), where both grew up, and, as their daughter Jeanne writes, paint "vivid pictures of a spirited time gone by." Joseph's begins in the period after World War I, and provides a portrait of the shtetl's various inhabitants. Bronia's memoir, which begins in 1944 and focuses on her survival, also depicts the town. Their accounts both complement and enrich historical writing on pre-Holocaust Jewish life. The Bekers' depictions of Kozowa and its inhabitants serve to challenge common concepts of the shtetl that have become rooted in American popular culture – the shtetl as an idyllic Jewish locus of traditional life or, at the other end of that spectrum, as hubs of anti-Jewish hostility.

The first dozen pages of Bronia's memoir depict a happy childhood in Kozowa, replete with lively characters and descriptions of local folkways. Born in 1920, she recalls the bucolic natural setting of the town, where the air was clean and children played by a little river. The account is devoid of foreboding: it recounts a carefree youth spent among friends and family, alongside non-Jewish inhabitants who posed no threat. The family was economically comfortable and, despite the lack of modern advances such as running water, life was good. She recounts the public bathhouse, pre-Sabbath baking and market days. Noting that "there were so many types of people in Kozowa that I could write a book just trying to describe them," she offers an homage to some of the more colourful shtetl inhabitants: Shikeleh the water carrier, Benzion the *shoychet* (kosher butcher) and his wife, Benzinachy, with her terrible memory; Lipah Tsal Abers and his cousin Hindeleh, who lived upstairs, who recited *Kiddush* (a Sabbath blessing) so loudly that he could be heard across the town; Tsache "the blecher" (tinsmith); Yankl "the stolyer" (carpenter), Malkeh "di Goylemiteh" (female golem) who never spoke with anyone; Shifraleh "porech" (dust) who lived in squalour; and many, many others, each with their own anecdotes.

Joseph Beker's memoir, originally written in a rich, idiomatic Polish Yiddish, also begins with a portrayal of the 225 families of Kozowa in all of their diversity, and wistfully depicts the traditions of the town, beginning with the Sabbath. He recounts his mother preparing *cholent*, a stew, inviting all the neighbours to bring their pots and offering a prayer to God that it turn out well. He remembers what it was like to go to the *mikveh*, recite the various blessings, observe the women's Sabbath activities and struggle to obtain kosher meat. Families were large, the streets were muddy, and there was no electricity or modern conveniences. The Jewish population occupied the centre of the shtetl and gentile peasants from neighbouring villages came into town on market days. Joseph recounts the roles of the Jewish representatives such as the rabbi, Hasidic *rebbe* and the seven *melamdim*, teachers, in the school. Like Bronia, he portrays the more colourful inhabitants of the town, such as Moishe the Cripple, Shikeleh the water carrier and others.

These character types and their world as portrayed by the Bekers form part of a vast culture in which the shtetl has long occupied a central position as the locus of traditional Jewish life. The inhabitants and way of life in the shtetl have been depicted in multiple contexts: literary works, art, film, musicals, photography, memoirs, memory tourism in the form of trips to shtetl sites or museum exhibits, and others. This lost world is familiar to any reader of modern Yiddish and Hebrew literature, where the shtetl was a favourite site for the pantheon of writers beginning with Sholem Yankev Abramovitsh (Mendele Moykher-Sforim) in mid-nineteenth century Russia. Abramovitsh and his fellow writers, who were proponents of modernity (the Haskalah), depicted a fictionalized shtetl in a critical light with the intention of drawing their readers away from a traditional Jewish life that they perceived as outdated and misguided. In their writing, the shtetl is depicted as in decline and obsolete.

The shtetl and its characters also appear in the array of popular culture associated with the 2.5 million Jews who left the Old World and the shtetl behind beginning in the last two decades of the nineteenth century, first for larger urban centres and subsequently for overseas destinations, notably New York. For these immigrants and their descendants, the shtetl evolved as an idealized symbol of a lost past, even as it continued to exist in the Old World. Between the two world wars, the shtetl appeared as a setting in a series of classic Yiddish films produced in the United States and Poland, notably the popular musical *Yidl mitn fidl (Yiddle With His Fiddle,* 1936), which was shot on location (rather than in studio) in the Polish town of Kazimierz with shtetl inhabitants cast as extras.

The destruction of Jewish life under the Nazis led to the sudden demise of the shtetl and its way of life, and a heightened memorialization of that lost world, notably in the form of *yizkor* books. While there had been a disconnect between the shtetl as a locus of Jewish life and the fictionalized shtetl of literature or the remembered shtetl of immigrant nostalgia, the shtetl continued to exist in space and time. The Holocaust severed these connections. In Jeffrey Shandler's recent work, *Shtetl: A Vernacular Intellectual History,* he refers to the shtetl "as an archetype of the mode of postmemory," where the relationship of the memory to its source is always mediated. The postmemory of the shtetl after the Holocaust is marked by a shift: "The loss of the remembered shtetl leaves its postmemory bereft of its defining element."[1] An example of this is the 1964 musical *Fiddler on the Roof,* which offers a simplified and sanitized representation of the shtetl that cannot be challenged by any real, existing version of it.

The Bekers contribute to the postmemory of the shtetl by revisiting the people that they knew in their home town as they were growing up. Their vivid portraits offer a memorial to a lost world. Their representation of the shtetl, which is anything but sanitized, offer a true testament to a shtetl that was abruptly snuffed out along with so many others.

Memoirs such as the Bekers' underline the impact of the shift from memory to postmemory. Joseph Beker indicates the existence of a deep culture clash between the culture of his childhood shtetl and the post-Holocaust world in which he raised his family: "When I try to tell my children these things [about the piety of his parents], they have no clue as to what I'm talking about, so, while my mind is working, I have written down what I can remember, and perhaps someone will be interested in reading it." In the process, he has crafted a postmemory for a world that has no referent and only exists in sources such as the Bekers' memoirs.

While both of the Bekers' descriptions of Jewish shtetl inhabitants may appear as separate from the rest of their Holocaust narratives, they form the core of the memoir: the moral imperative to remember a lost world whose inhabitants did not survive the Holocaust and who we, as the reader, now share. Both Bekers offer similar sentiments about their keen sense of having experienced a world that is no more, and they do so at the micro level by recounting their own recollections of individual people who occupied the shtetl. The reader cannot but be compelled by Joseph's words, "We cannot forget those closest to us, those with whom we grew up. We can no longer experience the

---

1 Jeffrey Shandler, *Shtetl: A Vernacular Intellectual History* (Rutger's University Press, 2014), 44–45.

life that once was, but life must go on…. How can we compare the Jews of Kozowa with the Jews of today? They are as different as night and day. We have to understand that is what time does." The loss of the individual characters in the memoirs marks the end of an entire civilization that today exists only as the collective memory of those who read it.

Rebecca Margolis
University of Ottawa
2014

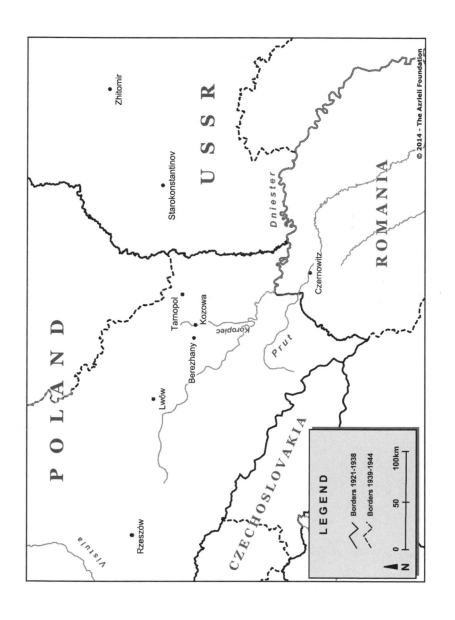

POLAND

Vistula

Rzeszów •

Lwów •

Tarnopol •
Berezhany
Kozowa •

Koropiec

Prut

CZECHOSLOVAKIA

USSR

Zhitomir •

Starokonstantinov •

Dniester

Czernowitz •

ROMANIA

© 2014 – The Azrieli Foundation

LEGEND

Borders 1921-1938
Borders 1939-1944

0   50   100km

N

Bronia's Story

Our Little Shtetl

On July 21, a beautiful sunny day in 1944, I found myself sitting in the ruins of our house, crying bitterly. The little town of Kozowa, where I was born on December 9, 1920, had been destroyed. After I could cry no more, I just sat there thinking and dreaming, watching my life pass before me.

My hometown, Kozowa, was in Poland (now western Ukraine), the area known as Galicia. It was built among meadows and fields of corn and wheat that stretched for miles. In my mind it came to life in front of my eyes like an oasis in the middle of a desert. I could see the centre of town where there was a marketplace with a round building containing three stores and two groceries. Around the marketplace, streets branched out in all directions. I used to love to run down the hill from the marketplace to my home. At the top of the hill was the drugstore, and as I ran down I would pass a fence, then the pump where we got water, and then our neighbour's house before getting to our home. After turning the corner and walking up a few steps, I would reach our big, brown front door.

I loved living in Kozowa. The summers were beautiful, not too hot or humid, and the air was always clean, making it a pleasure to take a deep breath. I used to go for long walks in the fields to pick wild flowers or just to get a little sun on my face. On a nice sunny afternoon in July or August, I would dress in a dirndl and sandals, put a ribbon in my hair and walk down to the train station with one of my girlfriends. It was a beautiful walk. We would take a short cut through the school-yard and then through a garden that looked almost like a park. The garden was private property but had a path that led to the Koropiec River. The water was so shallow that we could even walk across it. The riverbed was uneven and the water ran swiftly downstream, like a miniature waterfall. Over that waterfall was a little bridge. Well, that's what we called it, but actually it was just a board lying across our tiny river. We would take our shoes off and walk across the board in our bare feet.

On the other side of the river was another path between gardens – mostly vegetable gardens – where a herd of goats roamed. We often talked to the goats, and sometimes they even followed us. It took maybe an hour to reach the train station. We made sure to get there before three o'clock, when the train arrived. The station was a beautiful structure with an iron fence and a garden in back. We waved to the passengers in the windows of the train, and when the train left we walked home with the thought of coming back in a few days. Somehow I never got tired of that walk. I was always excited to go to the train station again.

When I didn't have anyone to walk around with, I wouldn't go very far by myself. I walked only to the river, where I'd sit down to read my book, talk to the goats or just listen to the birds. Sometimes peasant girls came to do their washing at the river. One might think this was hard work but it seemed to me, as I watched them, that they were having a lot of fun. They laughed, giggled and told jokes while beating the wash with a flat stick. I don't think they would have enjoyed themselves more at a picnic or even in a theatre. The girls had long braids and wore tight vests and long, wide skirts, with one hem of the skirt tucked into the waistband. They were barefoot and carried the wash on their backs or in pails. Walking to the river, they made up part of the beautiful picture.

Despite these idyllic scenes, life in our town was not all that glamorous. Maybe we didn't know better, or maybe we were just smart enough to make the best of it. For instance, we had no running water, so even taking a bath was quite an ordeal. If you were fortunate enough to have a tub in the house, you had to bring water from the pump, heat it in a big basin on the stove, and pour it into the tub. When you were done, you had to pour the water out again. This is why many townsfolk went to the public bathhouse to take a bath or even a steam bath instead. I don't know exactly how the steam was made – an old man, Ludz, attended to that. When the steam was ready, another old man, Mikola, went around the streets banging two scythes together to let people know it was time to go to the steam bath. This happened only once a week, on Fridays, when everybody had to get ready for the Sabbath.[1] In the afternoon, all the men left their work or place of business to bathe. The women went later, when Sabbath preparations were done.

Every Friday morning my aunt, who lived around the corner from us, baked cheese buns. They were the best cheese buns in the whole world, and she baked enough for a whole week. My mother, Malka Esther's, specialty was cinnamon buns. By noon on Friday, the buns were ready – first my mother gave me some cinnamon buns, then I went to Auntie for some cheese buns, and then I took them all to my grandmother's house. And what a lady she was! My grandmother was very neat and always wore a long skirt, high-laced shoes and a vest. She had vests in every colour, but especially loved to wear bright colours. Once, she bought a long sweater and, after trying it on, decided it was too dark for her, so she gave it to my auntie and bought a red one for herself. My grandmother's head was always covered with a clean, starched kerchief. She used to say that she wished she lived in

---

1   For information on the Sabbath, as well as on other religious and cultural terms; foreign-language words and expressions contained in the text; major organizations; significant historical events and people; and geographical locations, please see the glossary.

a town where there was no mud so that her shoes could always stay clean. In our town the roads and the side streets were not paved, so after it rained everything turned to mud. We had to wear galoshes or high boots.

My grandfather had died young, and my grandmother remarried. Her second husband passed away when she was seventy-five years old, yet even at that age she was by no means an old lady. She walked for miles and was always busy. Since she did not like being alone, nor did she want to live with one of her daughters, Grandma married a third time. Her husband was an old man who had a small farm on the outskirts of town. When she moved into his house his housekeeper, Marina, who had taken care of the household for years, was upset. Marina gave my grandmother plenty of trouble, but my grandmother ignored it and laughed. She knew that Marina was just jealous. In general, Grandma had a very good nature; she never worried about anything and was always in a good mood. When I brought her those cheese and cinnamon buns on Fridays, she locked them in a chest because she didn't want Marina to steal any. I loved to visit Grandma in that small, clay farmhouse with its straw roof. There were cows in the barn, and the property had a vegetable garden and a lot of fruit trees. I picked plums and cherries right from the trees. I'd spend the whole afternoon there until it was time to go and then Grandma would walk me halfway home.

Grandma loved her five grandchildren. My mother had two daughters – me and my sister Sarah – and Auntie had two girls and a boy. Grandma treated her grandson, Menche, a little better than us girls. When Grandma's brother in Canada sent her ten dollars, she gave the money to my cousin Menche so he could buy himself something. We were jealous, of course, but I loved her anyway.

My father, Moses Baruch Rohatiner, had been married before. His first wife had died in childbirth and I had nine half-siblings, three of whom lived in Kozowa. My father had a little leather store and our family was comfortable, though never rich. Because we had no running water, we hired Shikeleh the water carrier to bring water from the pump to the house in two pails that hung from a long pole resting on his shoulders. Every Friday, my mother baked a special little loaf of bread for Shikeleh.

There were so many types of people in Kozowa that I could write a whole book just trying to describe them. And nobody was called by his or her real name; everybody had a nickname. For instance, next door to us lived the *shoychet*, the ritual slaughterer. His name was Benzion, so his wife was called Benzinachy. What a character she was! She was a religious woman who covered her shaved head with a kerchief, as other religious women in the town did. Yet, somehow that poor woman always looked helpless. She was large, with an apron always tied around her waist, and her face was always dirty. For as long as I'd known her she had only one front tooth, and she was constantly chewing because it took her such a long time to chew her food. Benzinachy was a good woman who wouldn't hurt a soul. Many of her children had died young of various diseases, and she was left with only a boy and a girl. She and her husband also adopted a boy named Gedalieh. I remember once when I visited her, she sent Gedalieh down to the cellar to bring her potatoes and said to him, "Gedalieh, keep talking to me the whole time that you are in the cellar." When I asked her why he had to do that, she told me that she had preserves and jams in the cellar, and if he was talking she would know that he was not eating up the goodies!

Since her husband was a *shoychet*, he brought home cows' spleens and intestines for their cats, and we'd see the cats dragging them around the whole neighbourhood. Those cats were the healthiest and fattest in town. But poor Benzinachy, she had such a bad memory! If she stuffed a chicken's neck and sewed it up, she would leave the needle inside. When she went to the store, she would buy each item separately because she couldn't remember two things at once. She carried her shopping in a corner of the shawl that she always wore, but even so, she often lost the things she had bought on her way home. Whenever we found a small bag of sugar or any other item on the street, we would bring it right to her house because we knew it belonged to her.

Across from us lived tall, skinny Lipah Tsal Abers and his hump-backed cousin, Hindeleh, and her family. Both families shared a single house. Hindeleh, neatly dressed in a long dress, apron and white kerchief, walked like a duck and looked like a penguin. Her husband was a large man with a red beard. They watched over their little girl, Kreindeleh, with terrible anxiety. They were always afraid of her catching a cold, so they dressed her in several sweaters and scarves. As a result, she was always perspiring and catching colds! Hindeleh had a very ugly black cat. When I asked her why she didn't own a nicer looking cat, she answered that an ugly one would never be stolen from her.

When Lipah Tsal Abers said *kiddush* on a Friday night, it was so loud that the whole town could hear him. He was a *melamed*, a teacher, who taught small children to read the prayer book. He was also a matchmaker, and sometimes after he made a match and received his fee, he would say, "Children, I brought you together; only God should separate you." His wife baked the best, most delicious black bread in town and sold it to the neighbours. Lipah and his wife had three daughters. The eldest married a man who was looking after his paralyzed father. She couldn't stand the situation for very long and soon left her husband and returned home. The second daughter married Yossi "Pulkeh" (thigh), who was very skinny and maybe seven feet tall. They lived with Yossi's mother. He was a businessman, and his in-laws were proud of him. I often heard them say, "He is the only man in town who owns a leather briefcase." The third daughter was always reading books and studying Hebrew.

Srul Leib and his family lived next to them. He was a plain man, a butcher, who had many children. When the children were young, the family was very poor. There were times when they had only a small piece of bread in the house. That was when their mother told them,

"Children, if I give each of you a small piece of this bread, you won't have enough, but if I eat it all you will have a beautiful mother." And she did eat it, and she was beautiful. When the children grew up and could help in the business, the family was much better off. I remember watching them arrive at home in a horse-drawn wagon, taking a calf off the wagon and pulling it by the tail into the house. Their mother eventually became a businesswoman and travelled by train to the big city of Lwów to sell things. Once, she met a young man on the train who told her that she was beautiful. "I have a daughter at home just as beautiful," she replied, and she brought him home and married him off to her daughter.

Across from the butcher and his family lived Tsache "the blecher," the tinsmith, who fixed tin roofs and made gutter pipes and other things from tin. He often sent his wife to Lwów to buy the raw materials, but one time, she came home without the merchandise. She called her husband up to the attic so no one could hear them and showed him the great bargain she had bought – a man had sold her a precious stone worth thousands of złotys for only the little amount of money she had. It was a plain stone, of course, and that's how Tsache became poor.

Next to them lived our neighbour Yankl "the stolyer," the carpenter, who always fought with his wife. Yankl made all the chests and coffins for the town. He often said that the best season for business was after Christmas because the peasants, who ate little through the year, would have a big Christmas feast and eat so much that many of them would die from overeating. He worked very hard before Christmas, preparing coffins.

On the other side of the street, at the top of a small hill, stood a lonely little house. It was whitewashed, with a black shingle roof, two little windows and a high step into the house. In it lived an old, fat woman who kept to herself and never talked to anybody. We called her Malkeh "di Goylemiteh" (the female golem). Who knows what was bothering the poor old woman, but she seemed very miserable.

We children would try to talk to her when she was sitting on the step of her front door, but she would chase us away.

Not far from this house stood another little house, built of clay, with the same black roof that somehow looked less mysterious than the other. There, the door was always open and children were welcome at any time. The Rotiner Rebbetsin (rabbi's wife) lived there with her husband, who was a *melamed* and taught school-age children to read Hebrew prayers and Bible. When the *melamed* suddenly passed away, the children kept coming to visit his wife. She was old and tall, always dressed in a long black dress with a kerchief tied under her chin. One time, a wind caught her kerchief and moved it sideways – it remained skewed like that from then on. The Rebbetsin was a fun-loving woman who always joked and played with the children. Although she lived alone, she was never lonely. We used to go to her house straight from school, bring her little pictures or cut-outs, and she always hung them on her walls. We really had fun with her.

Close to Rebbetsin Rotiner's house lived Motti the baker. He baked bread, bagels and all sorts of buns, which his two sons carried in large baskets to sell at the homes of the wealthier people. One of his sons, Matys, was cross-eyed. We used to say, "He is looking with his right eye into his left pocket." He would walk our elderly rabbi to the synagogue every morning and evening. I always thought that was a beautiful sight. The rabbi was tall, with a long white beard, a broad-rimmed black hat, a long silk coat and white stockings to the knees, with his pants tucked into them. In one hand he held a walking stick, and with the other he held on to Matys. They always passed by our house on their way to shul and they enchanted me every time.

Shifraleh "porech" (dust) also lived in our neighbourhood. She was something else. Dirty? Unbelievable! She was a widow and had a daughter, Chanaleh, and a son, Zelikl, who was mentally challenged. He always wore a dress and walked around without any shoes. Chanaleh was a pretty girl, but I'm sure she never washed her face. They lived in a small room with only a stove, a broken table and a bed, which all three of them slept in. Shifraleh, however, was not poor; she was a businesswoman who sold apples in the marketplace every day of the year. When it was very cold she sat on a pot filled with red-hot coals to keep warm. What a sight she was sitting on that pot!

Shifraleh's neighbour was Itsik Avrum, the coachman. He drove a large wagon, transporting all kinds of goods to and from other towns. He also had a fancy carriage and drove people to the train station. Itsik had two daughters and one son. His son, Meilach, was also mentally challenged and spent much of the day playing with buttons. If you gave him a button he was grateful to you for life. One daughter, Beibeh, was short, bowlegged, and had a big head. The other daughter, Baileh, was a tough woman. She stood up on her father's big wagon and whipped the horses. She married a lazy man named Cudyg who didn't like to work, so she picked up passengers at four o'clock in the morning to take them to the train station while her husband slept in.

Another memorable person from my town was Chaneh Ziprehenies. Chaneh was an old woman who had a son, Chaimtse, and daughter, Gitl. Gitl married a gentleman and they had a baby girl together, but soon afterwards he left for America. Gitl's husband sent her money and parcels and came home to visit every few years wearing a straw hat, light suits, and brown-and-white shoes. Everybody could see that he was an American because nobody dressed like that in our town. He hung out in the tavern and treated whoever came in to a drink. He kept promising his wife that he would take her and their daughter, Dosia, to America. Gitl was patient, but the townspeople suspected that he had another wife there.

Gitl's brother, Chaimtse, was a carpenter by trade, but he didn't like to work. He was a clown – he would dress up in his mother's long dresses and a wig and chase the Hasidic boys walking home from shul. Those poor boys would run away, yelling that a crazy lady was running after them. More than once a boy ran into our house, hardly able to catch his breath from screaming. Once, Chaimtse dressed up like an old woman, knocked at our door and asked my father where he could sleep for the night since he had just walked in from another village. My father felt sorry for the "old woman" and was going to take "her" to Zlaty's house, where anybody could sleep over. Somehow, though, I knew that it was Chaimtse. I told my father my suspicion but he scolded me, saying, "Be quiet." I walked behind them and suddenly pulled that "poor woman's" kerchief right off. Sure enough, it was Chaimtse! My father was shocked. Chaimtse didn't wait to be told off and ran away.

Another thing that Chaimtse the clown used to do was hide under the benches in the *mikveh* and stay on until evening when the women came to bathe. There, from under a bench he would watch them – until one time he was caught by a young woman. He also played a trick on a girl who was leaving for Palestine. When she was ready to go, she noticed that her luggage was missing. She was so frustrated searching for it that she missed her train. Everyone, of course, guessed who had stolen the luggage – it was Chaimtse. He said he was in love with her and didn't want her to leave. She went a week later.

Finally, Chaimtse decided to marry Chani, who was friends with his niece, Dosia. Chani was the granddaughter of Dodzie Frage, the most prominent Jew in town and president of the Jewish community. A match like this was unheard of and would be a disgrace to her whole family. Chani, however, was a naïve girl and Chaimtse made her fall in love with him. He dressed up as a beggar, took a fiddle and serenaded her at night under her window. She sneaked out to talk to him, and when her mother asked her where she was going, she said she was going to give a poor beggar a piece of bread. They kept meeting secretly until at last Chani announced to her parents that she wanted to marry Chaimtse. Imagine how the family took this news! To impress them, Chaimtse started going to shul every morning, sitting across from Chani's grandfather to make sure he saw him. Chani's parents even sent her away to live with her aunt in a different town, but this did not deter Chaimtse. He followed her. This went on for a long time, until finally Chani's parents saw that they had no choice and decided to marry them off.

All the prominent people in town were invited to Chaimtse and Chani's wedding. At the head table sat Dodzie Frage, Chani's grandfather; Nachtse, her father; Yitse Kuter, her uncle; and Dudzie Zwerling, a rich man who owned the lumberyard. Next to them sat Chaimtse's uncle, the coachman Mayertse, dressed in his best clothing – a big fur hat, high boots and riding pants. His outfit was certainly different from all the others since more prominent Jews never dressed like this for a wedding. All the men wore nice suits, long silk coats and black velvet hats, and Mayertse stuck out like a sore thumb. After the wedding night, Chani said that she had the best husband in town, but after a few days she was crying because her husband was out playing cards and didn't come home for a whole night.

In the middle of town stood a big white house owned by Gitl "di Breytkeh" (the wide). People called it the "drive-in house" because you could drive a wagon and horses right into the house. All the salesmen who came to town slept there since Gitl had quite a few rooms. Gitl was a large woman with red hair tied in a bun at the back of her head, a face full of freckles, wide hips and stocky legs. One time, a tiny man, Zishaleh, wandered into our town. As soon as Zishaleh saw Gitl di Breytkeh, he fell in love with her. Zishaleh was a funny-looking man with red hair and a little red beard. He wore a jacket two sizes too big for him and a pair of high boots with turned-up points. He walked quickly, with small steps, and stuttered when he talked. Zishaleh wished to become Gitl's slave and promised he would never leave her side. And this is what exactly he became. He carried water for her, cleaned her house and looked after her dog, which was almost as big as he was. Zishaleh kept saying that in the very near future he and Gitl would marry. What a couple they made – you could have built a whole Zishaleh from just one of Gitl's legs!

All the people in town were like one big family. The ones that were a little better off gave meals and clothing to the less fortunate ones. Despite everything, we helped one another in times of need.

~

Every Monday was market day in Kozowa. Merchants came from other small towns and villages and put out their merchandise on long tables in the middle of the marketplace. Mendel "pekeleh" (the package) lived with his wife and son in the basement of the market building. At the market you could get everything from shoelaces to candies to bars of soap, materials for clothes ... anything you could think of. Farmers came to sell chickens, cows, wheat, corn, vegetables and fruit, as well as to buy what they needed. There was another special livestock marketplace where farmers bought and sold cattle and horses. After the farmers finished their dealings, they went to the tavern to eat and drink.

When I was young I had a great time on those market days. I would run around, sometimes hitching a ride on a wagon, jumping on and off of the back without being noticed by the coachman. I watched people bargaining and saw how, when a woman wanted to buy a chicken from a farmer, she lifted it and blew into its tail to see how fat it was. One man wore a red hat and stood behind a small table with an umbrella over it, playing betting games. He counted blocks or nuts while asking, "Even or odd?" People would guess and always lose money. When I was a little older, I had to help my father in his leather store on market day. We sold most of the leather to shoemakers who bought it to make shoes and boots. They bargained a lot. If my father asked for five złotys, a shoemaker might say "three" and walk out. I was supposed to see if he was actually pretending to leave as part of the bargaining or going into the store of our competitor, in which case I would call him back and my father would lower the price.

One day, in the middle of summer, I got hungry and left the store to go home and eat. My mother told me that we had some kasha and milk in the cellar. We had no refrigeration, but the cellar stayed cool and in the summer we kept much of our food down there. On the floor at the back of the house was a trap door that led to the cellar stairs. That day, I went down and left the trap door open. At the same time, my grandmother walked in and went straight to the back of the house. She didn't see the open trap door and fell all the way down the stairs and was knocked unconscious.

When I saw my grandma lying at the bottom of the stairs, I screamed as loud as I could. I tried to lift her up but couldn't. I screamed and screamed until our neighbour, Yankl the tinsmith, heard me calling and came running. Yankl helped me pull Grandma upstairs and we lay her on the sofa. Other neighbours came in and stayed with her while I ran to get the doctor. We had no telephone so I ran all the way, yelling that I had killed my grandma. I was so frightened. By the time I came back with the doctor, my grandmother had regained consciousness and seemed all right. She stayed in our house for two weeks because her bones ached and she couldn't move around very well. Even when she was well enough to go home I was so worried about her. She was then eighty-six years old. I couldn't sleep and kept thinking of her constantly, wondering if she was really all right. I felt that it was all my fault. I kept saying that I shouldn't have left that trap door open. About six months later Grandma had a stroke and died.

Meeting Josio

In 1934, I had finished public school. At fourteen years old, I wanted very much to go to high school, but there wasn't one in our town and my father didn't trust me enough to send me away to a big city all by myself. He was afraid I would get spoiled. So I stayed at home. I read a lot, borrowing books from our town library, but I wanted more.

Soon after, I was sent to attend a school for girls from Orthodox families. I didn't like the idea because I wasn't that religious, but to please my father I went. I actually learned a lot there and never regretted going. At that time I also belonged to a Zionist youth club, Betar, whose goal was to encourage us to go to Palestine and fight to establish a homeland. My father, of course, didn't know about it and would never have allowed me to go there. He was not a Zionist – he was waiting for the Messiah to give Jews a homeland – and he wouldn't have liked the idea that boys and girls were meeting there together. I didn't see anything wrong with belonging to the club. I had a really good time at the discussions, lectures and dances. There were many members in our town, and we met in the evenings and Saturday afternoons.

At Betar I noticed one boy, Itse Mass, who never talked to the girls. He'd sit in a corner and play chess with the older boys, or he'd read a paper, or just talk to other boys. I made up my mind that he was going to be my boyfriend. Itse came from a very nice family; his father was a bookkeeper and Itse worked in his father's office. Once, in the middle of a meeting, someone came in and yelled, "There's a fire at the other end of town!" We all got up and ran to see what was going on. People made a queue from the pump to the fire and handed pails of water to one another to pour on the fire until the firemen finally came and put the fire out. And there, without realizing that it was happening, Itse Mass, whom I had an eye on, started talking to me. We walked back to the club together, and from that evening onward, we met near the drugstore every night and went for long walks.

Itse and I talked about books that we had read and about people and the world in general. He was intelligent, smart and polite, and I really enjoyed his company. His father had a beautiful library at home, and Itse would sneak out books and give them to me to read. His father never lent books to anybody, so I always returned them before he found out. I read day and night. Afterward, Itse and I discussed the books that I had read. He never came to our house because my father didn't allow me to bring boys over. Although we really cared for each other, neither of us ever mentioned it. This went on for three years. During one summer, I visited one of my half-brothers who lived in another town and Itse wrote me such beautiful letters, in which he added short poems in Hebrew. He was very shy and I saw that it was much easier for him to write than to talk.

Then, one day after I returned from my half-brother's house, one of my girlfriends introduced me to a boy named Josio Beker. Josio was different in millions of ways from Itse. He was a handsome man, older, and sure of himself. He seemed so strong, not afraid of anything, like there wasn't a thing in the world that he couldn't do. He had everything that Itse was lacking. Itse was good company but he was a mama's boy who depended on his parents. I got the feeling that if anyone started a fight, he would have been the first to run away. Josio impressed me with his strength and his sense of humour. I liked that a lot, but we were so different, and our families were also so different.

We were not rich – my father was only a small businessman – but

I think that we were considered one of the more prominent families in town. Though I could never really understand why, shoemakers, carpenters and all the people working in trades were considered lower class. Josio's father, a shoemaker, had died young, and his mother was left with four children. She earned a living by selling fruit in the market. When he grew up, he provided for his family. He worked very hard so that his mother and siblings were not lacking for anything.

Although Josio caught my eye, my father would never have allowed me to go out with him, let alone marry him. So I kept meeting him secretly. When I was with Josio, I felt relaxed, secure and protected. It felt to me like he had never been young, having always worked to support his family. Though we didn't have much in common, I saw that he was smart and devoted to everybody close to him. I admired him for that, and I knew that being a good person was worth more than all the education in the world. I became quite serious about him and neglected Itse. When Itse found out that I had a new friend, he dropped me. He wouldn't even talk to me. It bothered me because I missed our conversations and discussions, but I had to make a decision. I couldn't have both.

~

While all this was going on, there was talk of war. I didn't fully realize what a war meant. Naively I thought that finally we would have some excitement in our town – soldiers would come and go! I was anxious to see what would happen. Then, the situation grew serious. All men up to forty-five years of age who had once served in the army were mobilized. Since Josio had served in the army in 1937, he was called up too.

On September 1, 1939, Germany invaded Poland and Poland was defeated in only a few weeks. The Soviets and the Germans divided Poland between themselves: the western part of Poland went to the Germans and the eastern part, where we lived, went to the Soviets. Many Jewish Polish soldiers ran south to Romania and from there went to Palestine, where they formed an army-in-exile, Ander's Army, to fight the Germans.

With Soviet troops arriving and settling in Kozowa, there were a lot of changes. The Soviet officials, even when they were poorly dressed and looked like peasants, were welcomed by the communists in our town. They threw flowers when Soviet trucks and soldiers passed, greeting them with open arms. But the new situation was not all peachy for the rest of us. The Soviets took over all the public institutions and arrested the mayor of the city and anyone who was considered rich or was a town official; they sent them all to Siberia. They nationalized the bigger businesses and shut down the smaller ones. Everybody had to work, but the poorest people got the highest positions in town. The Soviets didn't care if a man could do the job well – it only mattered that he was poor and working class. A man who used to sweep the streets became mayor and all the ditch diggers became white-collar workers. They were sitting in offices and living it up. Because my father was a businessman, I couldn't get an office job and had to take work at an ice cream parlour.

In the meantime, Josio came home. He wouldn't run away to Romania with the other soldiers in the Polish army because he knew that his family was alone, and he came home to look after them. We learned to live with the Soviets. It wasn't too bad. As time passed, the young people began to organize trips to the nearby city of Berezhany to see shows. In winter, we rented sleighs pulled by horses wearing little bells on their necks, and rode to Berezhany wrapped in blankets. On cold winter nights, we rode the sixteen kilometres to the city and back under a beautiful, starry sky. I just loved that.

Naturally, I soon got bored at my job. All I wanted to do was go to school. I was nineteen years old and eager to learn, study and find out more about life in general. When I found out that the Soviets were looking for somebody to send on a leadership training course for various government organizations, I saw this as an opportunity. I really didn't care what kind of course it was or what I was going to learn there – that's how badly I wanted to go to school. I applied and was accepted.

My father obviously didn't approve of me going off by myself. Fortunately, one of my half-brothers took my side and influenced my father, convincing him that it was all right for me to go and that I could take care of myself. I was very excited. Lwów, where the school was, was a beautiful, big city. My brother accompanied me there and found a family with whom my parents were friends. I was supposed to go there for dinner every day so that I wouldn't eat non-kosher food. At the school, I met many boys and girls my age. After being assigned to my class, I started to look for a place to live. On a wall in the corridor, I saw an ad posted for a room suitable for two girls, with reasonable rent, close to school. While I was looking at it, I met an older, married girl from my hometown who was attending the same school and also looking for a room. We went to see the room and decided to rent it. It was in a beautiful house that looked like a little castle in a gorgeous neighbourhood. I loved it.

Each day, I walked to school, and took a streetcar from there to the family friends with whom I dined. They had lived in Germany for many years but after Hitler came to power they were forced to leave and found refuge in Lwów, which was under Soviet control. Many Jews who lived in the western part of Poland, which was occupied by Germany in 1939, had left their homes and come east to live with the Soviets, which was, at the time, a safer option for Jews. Before I left Kozowa, I, too, had met these refugees from the west; they had been issued documents that stated that they were not allowed to leave town or go to a big city. Among those refugees were a lot of nice young men who were once prominent citizens of Poland. They had left home with nothing, and of course it was hard for them to live in our small town. Some came to our house for dinner or just to sit around and keep warm on the cold winter days. They lived in vacant stores or anywhere they could find shelter.

One of those refugees, whose name I can't now remember, spent a lot of time in our house and became a good friend of mine. He was short, intelligent and had a beautiful singing voice. He got along well with my mother and kept asking her to persuade me to marry him. When I left for school in Lwów, I answered his letters to me. In the spring of 1941, he decided to surprise me and visit. As soon as he got off the train in Lwów, the police arrested him and took him to the police station because his documents forbid him from coming to the city. He was transferred in an open truck from the station to jail but not before he had a chance to drop a note on the road with my name and address on it. A passerby must have felt sorry for him, picked up the note and brought it to me. The note said they were taking him to jail and asked if I could help get him out. I felt terrible for him. I was afraid that the Soviets would send him to Siberia and he would be lost there.

That same day, right after finishing classes at school, I found a lawyer. He advised me to get a certificate from a physician in Kozowa stating that my friend had been sent to see a specialist, and the lawyer promised to see him and defend him. I also needed all kinds of documents from the Soviet authorities. I ran around a lot and got all the necessary papers from home through my sister, Sarah. While all this was going on, I didn't do my homework. I imagine that my professors thought that I had suddenly lost my head.

Finally, the day of the trial came. Instead of going to school, I went with the lawyer to court, and by some miracle my friend was freed. He had to promise to never come to Lwów again. The lawyer said that very few people were this lucky. I took my friend straight to the railway station. He said that he didn't mind going through all that because he got to see me after all! But after that I had to work extra hard as exams were coming up in June and I had a lot to catch up; I stayed up studying many long nights.

While I was in Lwów, Josio came to the city on business, and of course he came to see me. He waited for me at school, and all my new friends envied me for having such a handsome boyfriend. He took me out to beautiful restaurants for dinner and dancing, and we went to the great Polish theatre to see operas and other performances. From that point on, I saw him almost every weekend. I really looked forward to his visits. Sometimes he surprised me and just showed up unannounced. Once, my roommate and I had tickets to the opera to see *Eugene Onegin*. We were getting ready to leave when in walked Josio saying, "We are going dancing tonight." I argued, of course, that I already had plans to see the opera, but naturally he won me over. My roommate called up a friend, who took my ticket with pleasure, and I went dancing.

～

I was relieved when our exams were over, and I tried to rest up for a few days before returning home. Before I had a chance to leave, on June 22, 1941, my roommate woke me up at two o'clock in the morning, "There's a lot of noise outside," she exclaimed. We opened the window and saw a crowd of people running and shouting, "It's a war!" The Germans had crossed the border and started a war with the Soviets. I was very scared, being so far away from home, and I worried that Lwów would be a target for bombing. We started to pack so that we'd be ready to get to the train station and go home as quickly as possible.

The next morning, one of Josio's brothers came over. I was so glad to see him that I cried. He told me that Josio had been mobilized to the Soviet army and had to leave right away, so he had sent him to Lwów to bring me home. We took our suitcases and left, following him. He hailed a carriage and asked the coachman to take us all to the train station. When we got there, however, we found out that the trains were not running. My roommate and I sat on our suitcases, worried. Josio's brother told us he would look for some kind of transportation home and left us, promising to return as soon as he could.

We sat there at the train station the whole day but he never came back. In the evening, a passing coachman felt sorry for us and offered to give us a lift. I asked him to take us to my family friends' house. After staying there overnight, we decided to leave our suitcases and go to the school, hoping to find a way home. We started walking because the streetcars weren't running either. It was a long walk. All of a sudden, an air attack started. I saw bombs falling as we rushed into the nearest building. We ran, with others, down to the bomb shelter, which was really just a cellar, and sat there for quite a long time. When everything was quiet we walked out to find the building next door completely destroyed.

We walked again for maybe an hour, and then got very hungry and went into a restaurant. We had no money, but the owner gave us some spaghetti, which was all he had left. Finally, we arrived at the school. A lot of students, all from out of town, had gathered there and together we all decided to walk home. A few boys were going in our direction and we teamed up with them. I called up the people with whom I had left my things and told them I was going back to Kozowa. They begged me to stay with them, warning me that the roads were dangerous. But I knew that my mother would be terribly worried about me and that I had to go.

Kozowa was one hundred kilometres away and it was a very hard journey. Sometimes a farmer gave us a lift for a few kilometres. At night we slept in barns and some nice farmers gave us food. It took three days of travelling until we came to the neighbouring city of Berezhany, only sixteen kilometres from home. Since a lot of people from our town shopped there, there were daily coaches that carried passengers back and forth. I met a neighbour who was very relieved to see me. She told me that my mother was sick with worry about me, thinking I had been killed in the bombing. As soon as she saw me, she went back to tell my mother that I was alive. I left with the next coach and when I arrived at the outskirts of town, almost half the town was there to greet me.

I Saw No Hope

I was so glad to be home. I thought my worries were now over, but in reality, events were just beginning. Josio was in the army and most of our young men were gone. My family was intact – my three half-brothers were all living in Kozowa and my sister was at home.

Within about a week, the Soviets began to retreat. At the beginning of July 1941, German soldiers arrived in our town. The Germans had headquarters in Berezhany and would come into Kozowa almost every day with different demands. We were terrified of them, having heard stories from the Polish Jewish refugees about how they had been treated under occupation. Everybody started to build bunkers in hidden locations around town and whenever we saw the Germans, we all hid.

Soon, the Germans appointed a committee of prominent Jews, the Judenrat, and dealt only with those on the committee. Then, on German orders, the Ukrainian police took over the town to enforce the new German commands. At first they forced all the Jewish girls to work, loading us up into large wagons and bringing us to various locations to sweep streets and work in the fields. They beat us whenever they felt like it. At the end of the day we had to walk home. Just a few months later, the Germans formed a ghetto and ordered all Jews to move into one section of town. We were lucky that our house was in that section so we remained at home, but one of my brothers who lived in a different part of town had to move in with us together with his wife and three daughters. We had little food left. Life became sheer hell.

At the end of September 1941, a few days before Yom Kippur, the Germans ordered all men from eighteen to sixty years of age to be at the schoolyard at eight in the morning of October 1, Yom Kippur. Unfortunately, within those few days Josio had come home. He had been interned as a prisoner-of-war but had managed to escape and reach his family. On Yom Kippur, Josio went to the schoolyard, along with my three brothers and all the other men in town. It was impossible to evade the order – the Germans had threatened that the families would suffer the consequences if even one of the men didn't show up. When all the men were assembled, soldiers in uniforms arrived, drunk. They picked certain men out from the crowd – one picked men with glasses, another chose those with beards, another, men with delicate hands, and so on. They selected three hundred men in total, herded them into the jailhouse and told the rest to go home. They took two of my brothers; only the eldest came home. The next morning, those men were loaded onto trucks and driven away.

We thought the men had been taken to camps to work, but we found out later that they were driven to the nearby forest and shot. It's hard to describe how broken up our family was. My father was seventy years old and had to take care of all the children left behind. One brother left a wife with three children, the other a wife with two small children. Josio was lucky to have survived, and I was so glad to have him around. He helped us by bringing food and building another bunker. My father insisted that we shouldn't all hide in one place; that way, if one bunker was found, maybe the people in the other would survive.

~

The Nazis often came into town and shot randomly at any Jew in sight. They also started to search houses for hiding places and took the Jews they found to the town square. Then, when they decided that they had enough people, they walked them all to the cemetery, where peasants had dug graves the day before. Everybody had to strip naked, and the Nazis shot them one by one and kicked them into the mass graves. When the Nazis left town, we came out of our hiding places to learn who had been caught and who remained.

After every such shooting, the Germans commanded us to make the ghetto smaller. Many people lived in one room and, with very little food, we grew weak and less resistant to disease. An epidemic of typhus broke out and my mother and I got sick. My sister tended to us, but somehow she didn't catch it. When Josio visited he brought a friend, a Ukrainian doctor, to help us. The doctor inoculated Josio so he wouldn't catch typhus. I had a high fever. Most of the time, I was unconscious and didn't know what was going on around me. It was during that time that my mother died. Although she was in the bed beside me, I didn't know.

When my fever went down and I got better, I opened my eyes to find out that my mother had died a week earlier. I can't describe how I felt, though I imagine that anybody who loses a mother of only fifty-three years of age feels the same. Then again, a mother's age never really matters. At any age you have the same feeling for her – even if she is one hundred. A mother is never old enough to die.

Life without Mother was very hard. She had always been the true head of our household. Though my father was the provider – he kept us under his wing, educated us, saw that we were not spoiled, taught us right from wrong and tried to instil in us his Orthodox beliefs – it was Mother who really looked after us. When we did something my father didn't approve of, she was always on our side. In a way she pampered us, seeing to it that we had everything we possibly needed. She was a good person, always helping anybody in need. Though not educated, she was an excellent housewife. Our house was always sparkling clean and she made the best meals under the sun. She was my mother, and this is a good enough reason for me to miss her, still.

Now, my sister, Sarah, took over the household. She was beautiful, with big blue eyes, a lovely figure and gorgeous legs. She went out with the best boys in town, always in the high society crowd. Sarah wouldn't go out with just anybody – he had to be educated, well mannered and from a prominent family. She was proud, and few people were good enough for her to associate with. I could hardly believe how she looked after Father and me and cared for us. Even when we somehow got hold of one chicken, she was able to stretch it out into eight meals.

Throughout 1942 the Germans killed and deported Jews. The ghetto became smaller. We all lived in one room with my eldest half-brother and two of his daughters. He, his wife and all three daughters had been caught and loaded onto a train to a concentration camp, but my brother and his two older daughters managed to jump off the train and come home. My other brother's wife and their three children also lived in the same room. The situation was so bad that we saw no hope of surviving.

Rumours circulated that the Nazis would very soon come to kill us all, and so we started building better bunkers. Josio came to help us build, or rather dig, our bunker. Also helping us were some other young men still left in the ghetto. In our cellar, we dug a hole about six feet long, four feet wide and six feet deep. We covered it with boards and earth so that it looked like the rest of the cellar, but we left a square hole big enough for a person to go through. We then fitted a wooden box full of earth to cover that opening. Wires were put through the side of the box for use as handles, and when we went down into the bunker we pulled the wires down. The opening was covered and it was impossible to see the entrance to the bunker. Even if one looked hard, nobody would have suspected that a bunker was there.

One day in April 1943, a few days before Passover, the Germans surrounded the ghetto. Always on the lookout, we saw what was happening. In general, we slept very little, walked around at night on alert, and never got undressed to go to sleep. That day, we all ran down to the bunker, where we had food already prepared and cots to lie on. On a previous occasion, we had stayed there for two days and the Germans had gone through the house without finding anybody. On that day in April, ten of us went down: me, my father and sister, my half-brother with his two daughters, and my sister-in-law and her three children. After about six hours, we heard heavy boots running down the steps to our cellar. They were looking for us, digging.

We held our breath and didn't move for about half an hour, until they left without finding our bunker. But the pipes through which we got air must have gotten covered during their digging. We couldn't breathe. I was the weakest of all of us because of the typhus that I had just barely recovered from. I remember seeing my father sitting on the floor in his prayer shawl, praying, and my brother with a hammer in his hand trying to open the entrance to the bunker. Then I fell down and everything went black.

When I woke up or, rather, when the doctor brought me out of my unconsciousness, I opened my eyes and saw many people around the bed in which I was lying. My cousin Cyla was beside me. The first thing I asked was, "Where is my sister Sarah?" When I saw the looks on their faces, I understood that she was gone. Everybody in that bunker except for me, all nine of them, had suffocated. I was alone.

I became wild with grief. When the doctor tried to give me an injection to calm down I grabbed him by the throat, wanting to kill him for bringing me back to life. I had felt so peaceful while sleeping, and it seemed to me that I had been woken from a good, sound sleep to face a dreadful life, alone and terrified. I could hardly move my right foot, which was very swollen and had a big sore where my garter had been holding my stockings. Because I fell first and was face down, I was close to the ground where there was still oxygen while everybody on top of me struggled for air. Somehow I survived, but I could taste the lime floor in my breath for a long time afterward.

I had been unconscious for about twenty-four hours. I was told that the day after the Germans left, my aunt got out of her bunker and, knowing where ours was, came looking for us. She opened it and called, but no one answered. She found everybody dead. Some neighbours started to pull out the bodies one by one. When they pulled away the body on top of me they tore away my garter, which had dug itself into my swollen flesh and left a wound on my leg.

When Josio came into my room he was stunned. I will never forget the look on his face – he could not believe that I was alive. I couldn't understand it myself. I believe it was fate. From then on, Josio took care of me. I was completely helpless and couldn't walk because of my sore leg. I would never have survived on my own and didn't care at all. On that horrible April day it felt as though I had lost everybody. Only Josio had survived. He told me that the Germans had caught a thousand people, told them to dig their own graves, and then killed them all. Then the Nazis made the ghetto smaller yet again.

As I lay in bed, watching the peasants come into the house to take what they wanted, I thought how dear every little item had been to my mother, how she had collected those things over the years, how she had kept everything. It was a horrible experience, lying there in bed wanting to die, to go to sleep and not wake up. But Josio wanted me to live, so I did. He still had his mother, brother and sister, and their house remained within the new border of the ghetto. He gave me a small room at the back of his house and I moved in, taking the bare necessities and leaving the rest.

I could not figure out why he wanted me. He was so handsome, so good, so everything. He was all a girl could dream of. He could have had his pick of the most beautiful girls in town – there were still a few left – but he wanted me. He took such good care of me, better than a mother would. I lived in that little room in Josio's house for a month. Life was unbearable, but I thought, I can't keep crying and being a burden to Josio, so I told myself that I was away from home on a vacation and would soon be together with my family. Really, I saw no way out, no way of living through that hell. But Josio could get out of the worst situations, and he never gave up.

One day, Josio came running into the house. "The Germans are back in town!" He quickly picked me up and ran, his mother and sister following. We reached the fields outside the village and stayed there the entire night. In the end, we found out that it had been a false alarm, and came back. It was nevertheless clear that we just couldn't live like that anymore. Josio started to look for farmers who would take his mother, brother and sister. He found a few who were willing, but he couldn't trust just anybody. Finally, he found a very nice man, someone he had known for years, who was willing to keep them in a hiding place in his house. Josio and his brother then bought two bullets, thinking that if they were caught they would shoot one German and leave a bullet for themselves.

In the meantime, life in the ghetto became even more unbearable. The Nazis came to town more often, making all kinds of demands. We could tell that the end of the war was near and they were getting desperate. I didn't worry at all. I was not afraid anymore because I just didn't care what happened to me. But Josio did. Josio was making plans with his close friend Kawalek, a dentist, who still had a fair bit of money. The two were very fond of each other. Kawalek had a Protestant friend named Gnidula, who had once said to him, "If things go really badly, come to me and I will keep you hidden in my house."

One day, in the middle of May, Josio and Kawalek took Gnidula up on his offer. They went to Gnidula's farm to build a bunker in his barn for us to hide in. They worked for two days, building the bunker under a chicken coop, and then came home. We stayed in the ghetto for two more weeks and then heard an announcement that it was to be liquidated. After June 1, 1943, no one would remain. The Germans were coming to take everybody away. After that date, anyone seen would be shot. We knew that the time had come to leave. Whoever had a place to go, left, and the rest remained, waiting....

I will never forget the exodus from Kozowa. I was leaving everything behind and yet, we were lucky to have a place to go. We sneaked out in the middle of the night so no one would see us. We feared not only the Germans, but also the Ukrainians who lived all around us – they were our greatest enemies after the Germans. Some of them were always ready to point a finger at us, catch us, or even kill us themselves.

We left the house and everything in it, leaving the door open. All I took with me was a sheet, a skirt, a coat and pyjamas. We walked for a long time, reaching our destination before sunrise. When Gnidula saw me and Kawalek's wife he was furious. He wanted to take just the men, not the women, and it took a lot of persuasion before he finally agreed to let us stay. I thought that we were in heaven – Gnidula's house stood all alone in the middle of a beautiful field with green grass all around. He was a gardener and he had a strawberry field nearby. It was so very peaceful, a lovely day in June. The sun was shining, everything was green, and I could have stood there forever. But all that beauty was not for me. I had to hide, bury myself somewhere. When I crawled into our bunker I felt safe. I didn't think that perhaps I was seeing daylight for the last time in my life, or that maybe I would never be able to feel sunshine again or breathe fresh air. It's hard to believe that I was actually happy to be there in the bunker, yet I was. I was thankful to be hidden from the eyes of evil men and to be together with Josio.

The bunker was a dark hole in the ground with an entrance through a camouflaged opening from the chicken coop. In the barn, there was a wall with wheat stacked against it, so when someone came into the barn, only the wheat was visible. We spent our nights in a narrow spot in the barn and moved around a bit in the morning, exercising before going to spend the day in the bunker, where we could only sit or kneel. At night we covered our feet with blankets and for light used a small bottle filled with kerosene and a wick. We played cards to pass the time. Gnidula came once a day to bring us food and tell us the news. He brought me a notebook and a pencil so I could write my thoughts and feelings. He wanted to know what it felt like, being buried alive. I wrote little poems for him, which he always enjoyed reading. I also knitted him a sweater. Every day he left a pail of water in the barn. We washed ourselves even on the very cold days when the water froze. Somehow, despite the ice water, none of us ever caught a cold.

We stayed in Gnidula's bunker for nine months, never raising our voice above a whisper and learning how to sneeze without making a sound so that no one would know we were there. We had to be careful that people who walked by the barn didn't suspect anything because some of them wouldn't have hesitated to call on the Germans. Gnidula kept us well informed about the events of the war. The front lines kept moving closer to us and we had high hopes of surviving. In March 1944, about thirty kilometres from us, the front stopped and remained in one place for a whole month.

We kept waiting for the Soviets to liberate us, but sometimes we couldn't stand it any longer. We felt disgusted, angry and nervous, and we started to fight amongst ourselves. On calmer days we would tell each other our dreams and wishes. I wished that I could go over to a well and drink as much water as I wanted and walk with the wind blowing through my hair. Josio wished that he could cut a piece of bread from a whole loaf. Kawalek wished to drink from a clean, shiny glass. We kept making wishes and playing games and hoping that someday this would all end. When our spirits were low we prayed not to wake up. It would be so easy just to stay asleep forever without thinking.

Never Give Up

On the night of March 17, 1944, we heard noises outside Gnidula's barn. We sat in the bunker and held our breath, like we usually did when someone was near. We heard a knock on the door of Gnidula's house and heard men asking directions. After a few minutes, we heard a gunshot and people running away. Immediately, Gnidula's wife came to the barn and told us that Gnidula had been shot. She asked us to come to the house, hoping that we could still help him. Josio went with her, but it was too late. Gnidula was dead. His killers were banderowcy, Ukrainian revolutionaries who were anti-Soviet. Gnidula was a communist and had been telling those Ukrainians that the Soviets would return and everybody would pay for their crimes. When the banderowcy saw that the Soviets were near and the Germans were backing out, they figured that Gnidula might report them and put them in danger. After they killed him, they told his wife to take their three-year-old son and leave. She told us that we better get out too.

It's impossible to imagine how we felt – we hadn't walked for nine months and we had nowhere to go, but we had no choice but to leave our hiding place. As long as it was still dark, we had a chance to escape without being noticed. We put on our clothes and shoes and walked out into a dark, cold night. The snow had just melted and the roads were muddy. The Ukrainian killers were out there somewhere, probably on these same roads. Josio more or less knew his way around, so we planned to go back to our hometown. We hoped that one of our Christian friends would give us shelter.

We walked for hours, reaching the outskirts of Kozowa at daybreak. Kawalek said that he had a friend who would take him in so we parted ways and he and his wife left. Josio and I were afraid that when daylight came someone would notice us and we would be killed. It seemed like the military front was right there in front of us – everywhere we looked there were German soldiers! We soon spotted a barn with an opening over the door. Since we had to hide quickly, Josio, without thinking, picked me up and threw me into that barn and then climbed in as well. It was a big space with a little attic at one end. We saw a ladder, climbed up and hid between the bundles of wheat stacked up there. Our feet were wet and we were dead tired. While Josio was drying my feet in his armpits, we fell asleep.

All of a sudden, we were awakened by the sound of someone opening the door and climbing up the ladder. A plump middle-aged woman started to throw down bundles of wheat and when she reached the bundle next to me, without noticing me, she grabbed me by my hair. On realizing that she had touched somebody she became frightened and started to scream loudly. I got up and tried to calm her down, telling her, "Look, I am a human being. I have arms, legs, a face, just like you." She kept on screaming and told us to get out right away. I told her, "We are not going. We have to stay here until dark, because in daylight the Germans may catch us and kill us. I can't believe you would want that on your conscience." She left, though we were sure she would bring the police. We had no choice but to wait, ready for the worst. About an hour later the woman came back with a pitcher of milk and a loaf of bread. She told us to eat, rest and leave when it grew dark. It is hard to describe the goodness she showed. She made us believe that there were still people with feelings, with heart.

We stayed in the barn until dark and then walked out into the darkness without a destination, wandering through fields until we reached our town's cemetery. How we envied those buried there. No more running, no more hiding for them. I prayed that my parents, who were buried there, would take me to them. I felt that I would be so happy if only I were with them. But I was alive and I had to go on, and Josio kept reminding me, "Never give up." It was so hard – I wanted to go to the police and surrender. At least the Germans shot you in the head, and it seemed to me that to die this way was easy. I didn't want to fall into the hands of the Ukrainians, who had a reputation for doing terrible things. But Josio would not hear of it. "We must find a place to hide," he insisted.

Much to our surprise, there in the cemetery we heard voices. When we came closer we saw it was none other than Kawalek and his wife, sitting on the ground. Kawalek's friend, with whom he'd hoped to hide, was not a friend after all and hadn't let them in. We believed it was fate that we stay together. Josio remembered that a school friend of his, Wladek, lived in this neighbourhood, so he went to him to see if he would hide us. What a relief when Josio came back and told us that this man was willing to take us in! We went to his barn, which was full of hay. Wladek pulled out a few bundles and made a hole for us to crawl into and then covered up the opening with hay. We were all closed in, with very little air and almost no light, but we were glad to have shelter. Wladek's wife didn't know about us. Once a day Wladek sneaked food to us, telling his wife that he was going to feed the pigs. Indeed, half of it did belong to the pigs, but we ate it anyway.

After one week, German soldiers came to Wladek's house and set up headquarters there. The Soviet army was close by and the Germans kept retreating. We were sure it would only be a few days before the Soviets would come to free us. In the meantime, life became more difficult because Wladek couldn't get to us. He tried, but he was afraid that someone would see him. Once, when the German soldiers threw out some cabbage with meat, Wladek picked the cabbage out of the garbage and brought it to us. It was dark and we couldn't see what he had given us, but we were so very hungry. Maybe if we had seen the cabbage we would have noticed that it was spoiled, but we didn't care how it tasted – we were hungry and we ate it. We all got so sick, suffering from horrible diarrhea. I don't know how we lived through that night.

The next morning, the soldiers came into the barn and we heard them tell Wladek to empty the barn of straw because they were bringing in their horses. As soon as they left, Wladek told us to run away. We couldn't even wait until dark – it had to be in daylight. As sick as we were, with nowhere to go, we had to get out of there. German soldiers were all over town, but they didn't know or, at this point, possibly even care who was Jewish and who was not. It was our gentile neighbours we had to fear.

Kawalek and his wife left to stay with friends out of town. Josio told me to meet him at the house of one of his old friends, which was at the other end of town. We were afraid to go together in case someone recognized us. Josio walked first and I, a few yards behind him. I wanted to keep an eye on him to be able to see if he got stopped. I will never forget that walk. I tried to act natural, and when I saw a group of soldiers standing in the road I walked right between them, saying, "Excuse me," of course. I watched Josio in front of me, and then I somehow lost him but we had an agreement to meet at his friend's house, so that's where I was heading.

As soon as I knocked at the door, I knew something was wrong. I wanted to back away when a German soldier opened it and, smiling, invited me in. I said to him in Polish that I had made a mistake and had come to the wrong house. I ran outside and bumped into Josio's friend. He was surprised to see me. In fact, he didn't even know me. I told him that I was supposed to meet Josio there. While we were talking, Josio arrived, pale and scared. He had had trouble avoiding the Germans on his way to the house. We asked him to hide us somewhere but saw that it was impossible. The German soldiers had been staying at his house for six weeks and it didn't look as though they would leave soon. He showed us a bomb shelter, a trench really, that the Germans had dug in his garden and told us to hide there for the night since there was a curfew and nobody was allowed to be in the streets after dark. He promised to come in later to talk to us. We went into the bomb shelter, which was a long hole in the ground about four feet deep. We had to kneel in order not to be seen from the outside. This is the end, we thought. We saw no way out. The shelter was open and the soldiers could walk in any minute if there was an air attack. So we knelt the whole night, praying that the soldiers would leave. That night, we saw our prayers answered. By morning, we heard a command from an officer that everyone pack up and leave. We could not believe our ears. The soldiers had been staying there for weeks, yet it took maybe two hours until they had all left to move to a different post.

Josio's friend didn't come back to see us. Instead, the next morning he went to work. We were too afraid of the neighbours to leave, so we stayed in the shelter until evening and then tried our luck with another friend. This friend was glad that we were alive, but he couldn't hide us since he already had two Jewish children hidden under his barn. He told us about an empty stable not far away and suggested that we climb up to the loft and stay there until dark, when we could look for food. Again, we had no choice but to move on. We went there and stayed the whole night, but we knew that someone could find us at any minute, especially because the loft didn't even have a door. We thought of other friends, the Bajors, and decided that early in the morning, when everybody was still asleep, I would go there and ask for shelter. It was April and I was still wearing a coat and had a kerchief on my head. I said goodbye to Josio, not knowing what might happen, and walked away. I was lucky that nobody saw me.

I arrived at the Bajors' house and knocked on the door. Mr. Bajor had six children, and one of his daughters opened the door. I asked for her father but she said that he was still sleeping and asked me to come back later. But I was determined to get inside. "I can wait until he wakes up," I told her. Mr. Bajor heard us, however, and invited me in. Inside, I saw people lying in a bed under warm covers. I could not believe that such a thing still existed. How I wished to get under those covers and sleep without thinking! The lady of the house was very nice. They were all excited to see me – I had a feeling that they were almost glad – for they had known my parents and they truly felt sorry for me. First they asked if I was hungry, then Mrs. Bajor said, "I have five girls and you can mix with them. I will hide you from the neighbours and the Germans won't know. I'll tell them you are one of my daughters." They insisted I stay, but I told them that I was not alone. "I'm with Josio and I must go back to him right away. I hope you can take us both in." They insisted that I stay until dark and then go to bring him, too. I was in heaven that they agreed to take us in, but I remained firm. I had to get back right away because Josio would be worried, not knowing what had happened to me. Mrs. Bajor gave me bread with chicken fat on it, looked out to see if the road was clear, and I left. When I got back to the loft and told Josio we had a place to go, he was the happiest man on earth.

We waited until dark and then went back to the Bajors' house. In the meantime, however, the Bajors had thought about us for an entire day and had now changed their mind – they were afraid to keep us. Josio finally convinced them to let us stay for one month. We were sure that the Soviets would arrive in a few days since it was evident that the Germans were retreating and the Soviet front was very near. We still had some money and jewellery – Gnidula hadn't taken a penny from us – and we gave the Bajors everything we had. They took us outside to the backyard, where there was a hole that they had dug out to keep potatoes for the winter. From that hole, a tunnel led to another underground hole, where they had hidden things left with them by their Jewish friends. There were sewing machines, furs and various personal and household possessions. They pushed those items out of the way and told Josio to dig a tunnel from there to yet another hiding place. It was a square about six feet by six, with walls covered with straw mats and straw on the ground. Over us was their backyard. Mrs. Bajor gave us a pillow, a blanket and some food. We crawled in there and felt secure, thinking, Any day now, the Soviets will come and we'll be free.

For the first few days, the Bajors were very good to us. They brought food three times a day, like in a hotel. We were delighted and adjusted to living there. Our only problem was dealing with the mice, worms and frogs. There were ugly, short and fat field mice, long worms that crawled out of the walls and small frogs that jumped around after a rain. After a month, Mr. Bajor told us to leave. He'd agreed to take us only for a month and he saw no end to the war, so we had to go. When he left we talked about it and decided not to leave despite Mr. Bajor's wishes. We had no choice but to stay.

A whole battalion of German soldiers was stationed in the Bajors' house, causing more trouble for us. Mrs. Bajor could not get food to us with soldiers all over the place. Their field kitchen was right over our bunker, so we could hear them talking and, sometimes, when they were very close, we had to hold our breath. Mr. Bajor started to drink and was drunk most of the time. He never came to us and his wife could seldom sneak food to us. One night, when all the soldiers went out into the field for manoeuvres, Mr. Bajor appeared at our bunker, drunk, and told us to get out. He said that young, healthy people shouldn't be buried alive and that we should go to fight our enemy. I was afraid of drunks, but I left the bunker and declared, "Josio is sick, he can't move." It had been so long since I had been outside – almost three months had now passed – that the fresh air made me dizzy. Mrs. Bajor cried and begged her husband to let me go back into the bunker because the Germans could return any minute. Finally, he let me go.

One day soon after, Josio and I noticed that it was quiet. The soldiers had left. Mrs. Bajor told us that the Germans had run away and a Soviet patrol was now in town. Freedom was close by, but she advised us to remain in our hiding place until she let us know that the Soviets were really there and it was safe to go out. We couldn't believe it. We were so excited we could hardly sit still. In a few hours we heard a lot of noise and voices speaking in Russian. A whole crowd of Soviet soldiers were right on top of our bunker! It smelled like they were baking potatoes. We could hear Mrs. Bajor talking to them and suddenly I could wait no longer. I crawled out of our bunker and said to her, "Mama, I couldn't find it," and walked away. She told the Soviets that I was one of her daughters.

Now, I can't express what I felt then. I didn't even realize that I was free. I didn't think, I just kept walking straight home to our house, which was only a couple of kilometres away. I only felt that I was going home and everything would be all right, and that all that had happened was a bad dream. I had on a green dress. The mice had eaten some of it, leaving a hole right in front, so I wore a skirt over top to cover it. My long hair was tied back with a shoelace. I was barefoot and pale, but my cheeks were full. Maybe I was a little swollen. People stared at me as I kept on walking, toward home.

When I got to my house I felt as though someone had cut my whole body into little pieces. I wanted to scream, to shout, to cry. I did nothing but stand there. The house was in ruins. Only the foundation was left. A shoemaker who knew me well from when he used to shop in our store stood there, feeding his cow on the grass that surrounded the ruins. When he saw me he turned pale and shouted, "Jesus Maria! You are alive?" He grabbed the rope, pulled his cow away and ran home.

I sat on the stones for a long while. I was so very disappointed, so very hurt. I kept asking myself: Had all my suffering been worth it? Was it worth staying alive? What for? Nobody was left – no family, no friends. I felt that I was alone among so many enemies, so many strangers. I cried and cried, and finally decided that I had to face reality. I had paid such a huge price for staying alive that nothing could be quite as bad any more. I decided to close that chapter of my life, close the door on my past and see what lay ahead. I had a life to live and I was going to do just that. I was going to start all over again. I remembered that I had Josio and thanked God for that. I saw him coming toward me. We joined hands and started walking, ready to face the future.

Joseph's (Josio's) Story

We cannot forget those closest to us, those with whom we grew up. We can no longer experience the life that once was, but life must go on. The Nazis – may their name be erased – murdered my little sister, Esther, when she was barely nineteen years old. They also killed my older brother, Shmuel, and my mother. I will never forgive them, and will never forget. Go ask God why this happened. I would never have believed that the whole world would remain silent and do nothing. The world should be ashamed.

A Simple Life

I would like to tell my entire story, but I am not a writer and never even had the time to read a book when I was growing up. I remember so many details, which I am going to write about, but first let me tell you about Kozowa, the little shtetl in Poland where I was born, a small town that was not even on a map back then.

Kozowa is situated between Tarnopol and Berezhany, cities that now belong to Ukraine. If I close my eyes, I can still see all the streets and people before me. My father, Beryl, of blessed memory, died in 1927 when he was only forty-two years old, leaving my mother, Gitl (Genia), and their four children as though adrift on the ocean. My older brother, Shmuel, was sixteen years old, I was fourteen, my younger brother, Srul Hersh, named after my grandfather, was seven and my sister, Esther, was four. Srul Hersh and Esther were so young when our father died. They could not understand much at that time.

My father had been a shoemaker, mostly making soles and heels, but eventually he gave up shoemaking and helped Mother in the market, since she had a permit. I also helped her while I was still in school. After my father's death, we were left in poverty. I became responsible for my mother and the whole family, and I had to work to ensure that they wouldn't go hungry. I wasn't ashamed to do any kind of work as long as I could earn a few grosze, coins, but I always maintained my self-respect.

Not a week went by that I did not cry for my father. I remember him as a very honest, kind-hearted and pious man. He never once missed going to the nearby Strettener shul to pray and took us along with him to services. My father was a Strettener Hasid, a follower of the Hasidic group of the dynasty of Rabbi Yehuda Hirsch Brandwein of Stratyn in Poland (now in the Ukraine). Sometimes he would spend the Sabbath with Rabbi Mendel of Premishlan. He was strongly urged to send me to cheder, a religious school, and it was thought that I would become a rabbi.

My mother was born with a deformed hand, yet she was tall and considered an attractive woman. I read her the *tchines*, the prayers for women, every Saturday. She never neglected to say the specific blessings for washing her hands and for bread, wine and other foods. She had learned all this from my grandfather. My grandfather was also a Hasid and wore a *shtreimel*, the fur-brimmed hat of the Hasidim, and when my father married my mother, he was bought a *shtreimel* as well.

Every Jew in Kozowa prepared for the Sabbath, or Shabbes, in some way, and my mother, of blessed memory, began to prepare on Thursday. On Fridays, she was ready thirty minutes before the time came for lighting the Shabbes candles at sunset. Before the Sabbath, Mother invited all the neighbours on our street to bring their *cholent* pots over to our house, and she prayed to God to make the oven the right temperature so that the *cholent*, the traditional Sabbath stew that the women prepared for Saturday lunch, would remain hot until the next day at noon and not burn or dry out.

On Fridays, everyone went to the one bathhouse in town. Some went to wash off the dirt, while others went in honour of the Sabbath. There was also a *mikveh*, a ritual bath where one could immerse for purification. At noon, a non-Jew with a goat let everyone know that the steam bath was ready. I enjoyed going into the *mikveh* with my father, may he rest in peace.

On Friday nights and Saturday lunchtimes, we all sat at the table as a family. We made the blessing over the bread, said the other blessings commanded by God and sang *zmires*, Sabbath songs. Saturday afternoons, my father would take us by the hand to go to the shul to have *shalosh seudos*, the festive afternoon Sabbath meal, with the other men. We recited *Mincha* and *Maariv*, the afternoon and evening prayers, and the rabbi did the *havdala*, a ceremony to mark the end of the Sabbath. Then we went home and my father did the *havdala* for the rest of the family.

During Shabbes, Itsik Avrum's wife, who wore a *sheytl* (wig), came over to hear my mother read the *Tsena u'Rena* (Come Out and See), a Yiddish version of the Torah and commentaries that women read on the Sabbath. Afterward, they drank tea and talked about what was happening in town. They waited until the Sabbath was over at nightfall to light a lamp, but first they had to see if the *shoychet,* the ritual slaughterer, had a light on. This was a trusty sign that Shabbes was truly over, and only then could we turn on a light. It was hard for me to believe that after my father died I became the man of the house and I was the one to say *havdala*. Then the new week began, and everyone wished each other a good, healthy and prosperous week.

I also remember my mother reciting *Gott fun Avroham* (God of Abraham), a prayer that women recited for a successful week, before we lit our gas lamp. At the time I did not understand what fine, pious parents I had. When I try to tell my children about these things, they have no clue as to what I'm talking about, so, while my mind is working, I have written down what I can remember, and perhaps someone will be interested in reading it.

Kozowa, before the war, had a Jewish population of about two thousand, or around 225 families, according to my calculations. This number could be off by a hundred or so, but I think that my reckoning is correct. In those days, Jews were very religious and believed in the Torah commandment to "be fruitful and multiply"; as a result, many families had seven or eight children. I remember seeing all the children around with runny noses, the sleeves of their jackets sticky from their wiping their noses so often.

In the centre of Kozowa's marketplace, surrounded by small shops, stood our town hall, enclosed by a stone wall. The town hall was encircled by three rings of houses that Jews lived in. The first ring was made up of fifty two-storey houses, as well as some very small houses. My family lived in the second ring of houses, and then yet another ring of houses surrounded ours. Beyond these houses the non-Jewish streets began, where around three thousand gentiles lived. The streets were unpaved except for the main road that led to nearby Berezhany and from there to the larger city of Tarnopol. The rest of the streets in Kozowa were muddy. There were sidewalks in front of the houses around the marketplace, but once we stepped off the sidewalks, our shoes would be completely covered in mud.

Perhaps twenty or so villages surrounded our town, ranging from distances of four to seven kilometres. Peasants walked to town barefoot because it was a sin to waste their shoes by wearing them on a weekday. Market day was once a week, on Mondays, and thousands of people came to town, each one with something to sell, like chickens, butter or eggs. Stalls in the marketplace sold soap, and some sold chicory, which was used instead of coffee. I myself sold herring from a barrel. There were also some taverns where the gentiles drank whisky and beer.

Kozowa wasn't a wealthy town. We didn't have electricity or running water. Gas lamps lit our homes and streets and we drew water from wells. But in my day it was already becoming modernized and, with the installation of a pump, we no longer had to draw water from the well, only to pump it. There were many poor people in Kozowa, but our town also had a community of middle-class Jews who helped the poor. Aristocratic landowners in the Kozowa area, including one local aristocrat, owned large fields. During Passover, I remember him donating fifty baskets of potatoes to distribute among the poor so that they could eat *chremzlach*, Passover pancakes. In addition, they were given *matzos* so they were able to celebrate the holiday.

Some Jews owned a cow or two, which meant having their own

milk, and some had chickens for fresh eggs. Some also kept goats. My family had three cows, which produced about thirty litres of milk. My mother sold about twenty litres, gave two or three litres to the poor and the rest was for us so we always had cream, cheese and butter. We also owned three horses and about twenty chickens, some of which laid eggs. My mother had fresh eggs for us children, but only in the summer.

My mother often sent me to the *shoychet*, the slaughterer, to see if I could recognize our chickens in case someone had caught them and taken them to be slaughtered. Some people went around catching chickens, and I can't blame them – chickens, pigs and goats roamed the streets. I remember the pigs because Jews are forbidden to have pigs, so how did they come to be wandering around in the Jewish streets? Most probably, after the women had their chickens slaughtered at the *shoychet*, they cut them open and threw the intestines into the street, and pigs came to the Jewish streets to eat them.

Kozowa had a rabbi, a Hasidic *rebbe*, and two *moyre-hoyroes*, rabbis who made decisions on matters of rabbinical law, such as what to do if a chicken had a blemish in it. Hasidic Jews are only allowed to eat animals if they are free of any disease or blemish. If a woman cut open a chicken and found that the liver or the giblets had blemishes, she would run to one of these rabbis to check if it was still kosher. The school I attended was run by a *moyre-hoyroe,* and I heard the women ask him their questions. Who sees the insides of a chicken nowadays? Women of today buy chickens that are already koshered. In Kozowa, women lived differently.

Though we had a rabbi, a *rebbe*, two *moyre-hoyroes*, two *shoychets*, and six butchers, there was often no meat available because at the last minute, on Thursdays, all six butchers would contribute a little money and buy only one cow together to share. Jews are only allowed to eat the front part of the cow – we don't eat the rear half in remembrance of the story in Genesis of Jacob fighting with the angel, who injured his thigh. Then, if by an act of God, the cow became *treyf* (non-kosher) because of a blemish, the entire cow could not be eaten. As a result, there was never enough meat to go around. For Shabbes, when the women bought a kilo of beef, the butchers often argued with them and tried to give them bones instead of meat, but I recall that they still said good morning to each other.

~

Days in Kozowa began at five o'clock in the morning. In the winter months, when it was still dark, one could see Jewish men carrying lanterns on their way to study in the *beys midrash*. One was Shmuel Bronyes Shapiro, an old Jew with a beard who sold flour. If someone did not have money for flour to bake a challah, the special braided bread, for Shabbes, he gave them enough flour for free to bake a smaller *kulich*, a round bread, instead.

There were seven *melamdim*, teachers, in the cheder of our town. I can still picture them now. The first was the Rotiner *melamed*, who taught the younger boys the alphabet for one term. Then there was Yankle Shütz, who taught us how to put Hebrew words together. He was a little crazy and hit the children with the twigs of a broom. His wife, Elke Shütz, a good, honest woman, endured this hell. Their house, where we went to cheder, was small and very crowded. The third *melamed*, Frayim Leyb, was terribly poor. His cheder consisted of twelve children divided into two classes. Each boy was enrolled for one semester and was then sent to be taught by the *rebbe* if he learned well; if the child did not reach a high enough level, then he continued with the *melamed*. The fourth *melamed*, Berish Mandel, was an upright Jew with a yellowish-white beard. Also a poor man, he had to teach in the small, one-room synagogue because he did not have a house. Every boy had to bring a bundle of wood with him to heat the synagogue. The fifth *melamed*, who I liked to learn from, was Berish Reyze Adel. His wife sewed shirts and kept the house very clean. The sixth *melamed*, Lipah Tsal Abers, was a tall man. He had only one fault – he got flustered if someone asked him a question. He once said that I was a *sheygetz*, a hoodlum, and he hit me on my arm so hard that I still feel it to this day. He told me to be quiet about it, and I was afraid to tell my father because my father would certainly have sided with him. I didn't want to go back after that.

There was yet another *melamed* for the older boys who was also a *moyre-hoyroe* and ruled on religious questions. As a sign of respect, he was called Moishe Borukh Dayan, which means Moishe Borukh "the Judge." My father arranged for him to take me for one term. Every Shabbes morning before prayer services, I had to go to the *shoychet*, who was an extremely learned man, so he could hear me recite the Torah portion that I had been learning all week long. The *shoychet* gave my father a report and then I went with my father to services. I went to this cheder until I was fourteen years old and knew as much as the *melamed* could teach me. I don't remember the total of how much the lessons cost, but for me and my brother Shmuel he charged my father seven or eight złotys a week, which was a great deal of money in those days. I can't imagine how my parents paid this amount every week, but they certainly would have had to deny themselves food. They gave everything to their children. I will never forget how good my parents were.

My older brother, Shmuel, was a good student, quiet and well behaved, which pleased my father. Referring to me, the *melamed* told my father that a person who does not want to know is worse than someone who does not know. He could have been right; there were times when I did not want to learn. However, when my father died, I went to say Kaddish, the prayer for the dead, during the morning and afternoon prayers and kept up Jewish rituals.

My day began at 7:00 a.m. As I walked to school, I had to pass the Polish church and the Polish school, which started at 8:00 a.m. The *melamed* had told me that when a Jew went by a churchyard, he had to say the words, "Shakets teshaktsenu, veta'ev teta'avenu ki kherem hu" (You shall surely abominate and abhor it for it is to be shunned) three times. This is part of a biblical phrase from Deuteronomy (7:26) that warns against worshipping idols, and I certainly said it. I attended school until 11:00 a.m., and then I had to run home quickly because the non-Jewish boys threw stones at us.

When I got home, I got ready to go to cheder, where I stayed until 6:00 p.m. My mother sent my little brother, Srul Hersh, to cheder to study with the same teachers who had taught Shmuel and me. He also went to the Polish school, so he had a very good education. To this day, I am proud to have a brother like him. My little sister, Esther, was also given a good education in both a Jewish and a Polish school. She was a pretty girl and well behaved, truly a pure soul.

In our town everyone knew everyone else's business. Everyone had an additional name, like a nickname, that described who they were. For example, I was called Yoyne Leyb's grandson, and my mother was called Gitl Yoynes. In the marketplace, the tailors were Gadi Markus, Yossl the tailor who had no boots, Wolf Reichenberg and Tsale Bume Reichenberg, who was mute. The shoemakers were Leyb, Hershele Krafnik, Moishe Avram Izik's son-in-law, and Rakhmiel the coachman's son. A cooper who repaired kegs, a wheelwright named Berl, a scribe, a furrier, a glazier, three tinsmiths, two watchmakers, three hairdressers and a bathhouse attendant all lived in our little shtetl.

There were also the Kharaskever carpenters, Yankl and Leyb Stoller. Leyb made coffins and gave two złotys to whoever sent a non-Jew his way for business. In order to make the extra two złotys, some of the young Jewish men's wives would tell their husbands to get up early in the morning and hang around the marketplace in case someone came into town for a coffin. I know this because I myself got two złotys commission for sending a customer to Leyb for a coffin.

I remember that when two Jews met each other on the street, they wished each other a successful market day. You might think that they were conducting business, but no, they had to buy butter or eggs from the gentiles, and if they could bargain a little on the weight of the butter or on a few eggs, they had a good market day. If a Jewish man was unlucky and had a bad market day, his wife said that he was good for nothing. When someone earned a couple of złotys, his family could buy a large sack of potatoes and eat roasted potatoes the entire week and be happy. If your stomach wasn't burning with hunger, if you had enough to eat, you were content. That was what life was like in Kozowa. Life was simpler back then.

Pedigree or status also played an important role in shtetl life. If someone was rich, he was highly regarded, but if someone was poor, he was not as important as a rich man. But not everyone had pedigree, and those who didn't had a sense of humour about it. I remember all this because as a boy I would go to the *beys midrash*, the study house, and listen as people there gossiped. I remember the names of the few wealthy people because of the way poor people used to joke about them – like Raful "Pipik" (Bellybutton) or the Shmutzes, who were said to have one kilo of gold and the best food to eat. If a peasant brought a fat chicken to the market, they would buy it. When they bought meat they asked for the best white meat, while the poor people got the dark, which was as expensive for a poor man as the breast was for a rich man.

Once, as I was standing near a peasant woman selling chicken at the marketplace, a young Jew, Reb Moishe, took a chicken from the woman and blew the feathers on its underside. Then, he stuck his finger into the chicken's bottom. I didn't know what that meant, but I wasn't shy, so I asked him what he was doing and why. Reb Moishe's wife had taught him that you blow away the feathers to see if the behind is yellow, which means that the chicken is fat, and you insert a finger to see if you can feel an egg inside, because sometimes the chicken could be about to lay an egg.

So many different kinds of people lived in Kozowa. One was Moishe the Cripple, the son of Babche Yosheliks and brother of Shoel Shtatmir. The entire family dealt in lime. He was very short, and God had sent him a wife who was extremely bowlegged. It is difficult to describe a couple more well-suited. They lived – may I not sin with this description – like two crippled doves. God helped them, and the wife became pregnant and gave birth to a healthy child, and they earned a living. Their son-in-law made bridles and ropes for horses so they could pull the wagons. I don't remember how many children he and his wife had, but their home was below ours and they lived in great poverty.

There was another man in the same family by the name of Velvl Glicker, who also dealt in lime. You would think that the family would allow themselves to buy a wagon full of lime. Instead, they got together with five or six other lime dealers – we called them *kalichniki* – and bought a wagon full of lime, which they would then divide up. But they always got into fights that ended up in the rabbinical court. Then, there was the water carrier, Shikeleh, who carried two pails of water on a yoke over his shoulders for the well-to-do families that could afford to pay him. A non-Jewish woman brought us water twice a day, and I myself carried water. Our neighbour, Itsik Avrum, was an honest man who drove a wagon and delivered water in little barrels.

Everyone in Kozowa prayed and asked God to enable them to earn a living. That was life in our small town, and what every Jew was like in our town. They did not know any other way. How can one compare the Jews of Kozowa with the Jews of today? They are as different as day and night. We have to understand that this is what time does.

Making a Name for Myself

In a little town like Kozowa one had to learn a trade. My mother sent my older brother to become a carpenter, and she sent me to a shopkeeper as an apprentice. Shmuel apprenticed with a carpenter called Leyb, whom we called Leyb the hunchback. He was one of the better carpenters (he actually knew how to repair a piece of furniture). The shopkeeper I worked for was Bercie Isserles, who had a pastry shop and also made ice cream, which in Polish was called *lody*. As I mentioned, there was no electricity in our town, so I turned the *lody* machine by hand the whole day, for which he gave me twenty-five złotys a month plus food.

Bercie was a pious young man with three children. His son and one of his daughters did not survive the Holocaust; his other daughter moved to Israel after the war. His mother, Chaya-Sara Isserles, had a large business selling a variety of goods and kerosene. She sold everything wholesale, not to private individuals. All the shopkeepers from the neighbouring villages, as well as from Kozowa, bought from her. Since I worked for her son, she knew me well and asked me if I would come work for her. I said that I would if she paid me thirty złotys a month, and she agreed. This was a good wage and my mother was happy; she was also pleased that I was not running around the streets. She felt that they would make a mensch, a respectable person, out of me.

Chaya-Sara sent me to a small delicatessen patronized by all the aristocrats from the court, as well as the teachers, to buy ten decagrams of cinnamon. When I approached the owner, a man named Teitelbaum, he tried to persuade me to work for him. He had a better clientele and offered me thirty-five złotys a month. I really needed the money and thought that my mother would be even happier. I would be dealing with aristocrats, writing down how much they ordered for the whole month. When I brought out their order I had to kiss their hand, and they always gave me a couple of grosze, which I gave to my mother.

When I turned sixteen, Kozowa became a boring place to live for me. I wasn't happy with such a small life and I didn't like the business of kissing the hands of aristocrats. I had a great deal of pride. I would have liked to run away, but how could I leave my mother and my home? I decided I had to earn more money and not work for anyone else. I saved up about one hundred złotys and I took the train to Lwów, riding all night. Someone from our town put me up for one night and, in exchange, I churned fifty kilograms of butter for him. He mixed it with margarine, added a little yellow food colouring, and made bars of butter that looked like they had been produced in a dairy. Seeing the opportunity for business, I asked him for advice on how I could earn money. He told me that his family bought saccharine – which people used instead of the more expensive sugar – and sold it to peasants, making a very nice living. This was illegal, as saccharine was regulated by the government, but it didn't take me long to decide that I could benefit from the same trade. I bought some saccharine and took the risk of being caught and sentenced to a few years in jail.

I came home with the saccharine, sold it immediately, and became a merchant. I was soon making a lot of money and was satisfied. I gave the money to my mother, who didn't know I was involved in an illegal business. I also began to deal in flint for lighting fires. Flint was also part of the government monopoly, and if I were caught and sent to jail, buying my way out would be impossible.

In our town we used to say, "If the pitcher is full, it will overflow." And that's exactly what happened to me. I was caught with a rather large quantity of saccharine and flint, and I was put in jail. My mother cried a great deal, but there was nothing she could do. I remained in jail for five weeks. Instead of making my life sweet, the saccharine had made it bitter. I was only seventeen years old and was placed in a cell with an assortment of thieves and thugs.

One of the inmates, a seasoned crook, was the "commandant" of the cell. When a new man was brought into our cell, he was told to take an oath. How did the prisoners administer an oath in jail? They put a blanket on the floor and told the newcomer to stand on one corner; then, two thieves pulled the blanket so that the man fell on his nose and pretty much split his head open. I went through this initiation myself and will never forget it. In addition, I had to give over the food my mother brought me and endure the chief bandit's order that everyone play *dupak*. In this "game," someone is blindfolded and lies down with his buttocks exposed, then he is hit on the behind and has to guess who hit him. You can imagine that from a game like this, one's behind gets very swollen. Furthermore, at night the men didn't let me sleep because I was, after all, a Jew. I sat, I stood, I lay down. I soon got used to it, but it was difficult not to feel hatred toward them.

One day the jailer came in, called my name and informed me that I was free. I ran home, thrilled – but not for long. I soon received a summons from the court in Lwów. I went there on the appointed date, worried that my troubles were not yet over. The authorities, it seemed, wanted to find out where I had bought the saccharine. I stuck to my story, telling them that I had bought it on the street, but this was not good enough. They sentenced me to another two years in jail.

This time at the Lwów jail, I was a bit smarter. I bribed a policeman from Kozowa, Kalkin, and he came in regularly to read me any news from our town while all the people from town stood around him. In this way, I spent two long years in jail. Finally, when my older brother, Shmuel, was called up to serve in the army I was released.

The court had to let my family earn a living and with Shmuel gone, I had to be the main breadwinner and support the family. Now I was safer – the court had to free me and wasn't allowed to send me back to jail.

Now that I was done selling saccharine, I wondered what I would do next. We didn't have horses anymore, but I got the idea of buying a horse and wagon to drive around to the villages to buy and sell whatever I could. I had to support my mother, my brother and my little sister. I asked my mother to lend me twenty złotys. She was afraid that I might buy and sell saccharine again, so her answer was an emphatic "no." So, I pawned my Yiddish-Polish dictionary for fifteen złotys and bought myself a horse. In fact, the horse was so old that the owner had wanted to sell the horse only for its hide because the hide of a horse was worth fifteen złotys. So, I now owned one hide (what a terrible insult to my poor old horse).

Every morning, I went to our barn to feed the horse, but one day when I got there, the horse was lying down and could not get up. I called over a few of my friends and they helped me lift the horse. I stuffed him with anything I could to make him stronger and not have to put him down. Every morning it was an embarrassment for me to be seen with it, but in our town they used to say, "an embarrassment is not a shame." Still, I had to begin doing business. I borrowed my neighbour's wagon and drove out to Kryve, five kilometres or so from our town.

On my way to Kryve, I was stopped on the road when I came face to face with a gentile with a wagon full of grain. There was no way for both of us to pass, and because I had an empty wagon I had to get out of his way. There and then, my horse sat down on his behind and would not get up. I pulled and pulled at him until he finally stood up and I could drive to the small village. In Kryve, I sold a bundle of twigs and earned one złoty. That meant I could buy ten kilos of oats and the horse would have something to eat for eleven days. Though I felt unworthy to call upon God in heaven, I prayed to God to send me another bundle of twigs so I could earn another złoty. When it happened, I thanked God very much in my heart. Then I prayed to get home safely, that my horse would be able to take me there.

After this, I somehow managed to sell the horse for eighteen złotys and went into partnership with a young man named Gershon. He took me on as a partner because I made a living for him while he sat at home. He had two small horses that ran like devils and, with them, I showed him that I was a better salesman than he was. I would drive out for an entire week and bring back whatever my money could buy. I bought everything – plates, pots and baking pans. I shouted "fancy dishes!" on the streets of the village to sell them. Peasants came out of their houses to ask if I wanted to exchange firewood for oats. I had a scale to weigh them and knew the price – one kilo of firewood cost one złoty and a kilo of oats forty grosze. I exchanged all the dishes for oats or firewood.

One time, I was ready to drive home when a peasant came over to me and asked if I wanted to buy a fox pelt. He took out the pelt and showed it to me, and I insisted that it was really the skin of a dog. He swore by the cross and said, "You stupid Jew, you don't know the difference between a dog and a fox." In fact, I did know but I wanted to buy it from him cheaply so I repeated that the pelt was from a dog and bought the fox pelt for four złotys. He also sold me a sack of fish for five złotys, and a fat chicken. It was a Thursday, and I was glad that my mother would have fish and chicken for the Sabbath. I knew how pleased she would be.

I was very happy with the transaction and my partner, Gershon, was even happier. I sold the fox pelt for eighteen złotys, and Mother had extra fish to give the neighbours. She didn't sell them the fish because, of course, they had no money. To this day, I remember that fox pelt.

Not many boys in Kozowa knew their way around the villages like I did, and that's how I made a name for myself in town. I was very pleased when people began to call me Josio Beker, instead of Yoyne

Leyb's grandson, after my grandfather. I felt better about myself and was earning a lot of money. Once I had saved two hundred złotys, I figured that I could buy a good horse and wagon in the village and no longer needed a partner. I would work for myself and accomplish what I wanted on my own.

To start my own business, I went to the nearby market in Podhajce and met Vovche Banner, a horse dealer, who told me I should buy a young horse, a three-year-old. The horse was worth the price. I paid a hundred and fifty złotys, which was ten times the cost of my first horse. Everyone envied me. I had become a businessman all by myself, without a father, and I began to make bigger deals. I was no longer afraid to purchase larger quantities of goods. The bigger merchants took notice of me. In a word, I felt that I had become a mensch. I behaved like a gentleman and began to give to charity, and I no longer had to kiss anyone's hand; I couldn't stand wealthy people who oppressed the poor. I was only nineteen years old, and yet, I felt that I understood more about life than most.

The Polish Army

Although I was working and making a pretty good living, it was a heavy responsibility to support my family. I remember when my brother Shmuel came home, on leave from the artillery, wearing his army boots. He was serving for two years, but I wanted him to come home for good, to take over the burden of providing for our family. I had put aside a little money, and God helped me, but I did not want my mother to lack for anything.

When Shmuel did come home, I asked my mother what he would do. My mother told me that he could be a self-employed carpenter. He could make better privacy screens than others could and, if he found a customer for a coffin, he would make that, too. The only problem was that he had to have money to be able to buy lumber. My mother told me I should lend Shmuel the money and that when he sold the screens, he would pay me back. I did this, but from the ten screens he made, he sold only one. He had nowhere to store them and was forced to give up his business. Soon, he would have no choice but to take over my trade and support the family.

It wasn't long after that – I think either 1936 or 1937 – before I was called up for military service. Crying bitter tears, my mother accompanied me to the train to Tarnopol. She gave me an assortment of baked goods so that I would not go hungry. Whoever has served in the Polish army knows very well how people, especially Jews, were tormented. Damn them! After I had served for six months, I was granted a leave. While I was back in Kozowa, I discovered that Hershele Markfeld, from my town, was also serving in Tarnopol. His mother came to ask me to take care of him and to take some baked goods for him. Hershele was a mama's boy, but the Polish army would make a man out of him.

When my leave was over, I went back to Tarnopol. Of course, I delivered the package that Hershele's mother had sent him, and he was very grateful. I couldn't help him beyond that because he was in other barracks, but before long he was transferred to where I was stationed. Hershele was glad to see me. The next day, I asked him if he wanted to go with me into the kitchen for food. I had bribed the chief cook with a few grosze so that I could go into the kitchen before he had distributed the food and he gave me the top of the soup. Of course the fat, which was lard, was always on the surface, so instead of soup what I really got was fat. I let the fat cool down before spreading it on the bread ration, which was otherwise so sour that it was hard to eat. But poor Hershele was so hungry that he drank a whole cup of fat. He got diarrhea and had no time to run to the latrine. When I had to go into the latrine later, I saw Hershele cleaning up the mess he had made in the corridor. The next time I went to the kitchen with him, I warned him to let the fat cool down first.

Hershele was sloppy in his dress and was punished for it. I wasn't afraid of the army officers because my shoes were always polished and my buttons done up. The officers were always looking for horseshoes from dead horses to play a game with. Since I was tall, the officers chose me to play with them while my friends got to do fencing. It was a dirty game. I don't like to curse, but if a plague were to befall the officers and a fire were to consume them, I wouldn't mind. Whoever has served in the army knows what I mean.

Yet, life in the army wasn't so bad for me. Every week, my mother sent me a parcel with *rugelach*, a Jewish pastry. As I got to know the cook better, I gave him my tobacco in exchange for two dozen schnitzels. I ate some and sold the rest for fifteen grosze each. I also traded with bread. If you knew how to conduct business at home, you could also conduct business in the army. I got used to the military life and bought myself a fine army hat and epaulettes. At night I looked like an officer and not just a recruit. When I went into town, the soldiers thought that I was an officer and saluted me!

I always thought of my mother, my brothers and my only sister, whom I loved very much. Quite simply, I missed them. I decided to ask for an eight-day leave so I could go to Kozowa. I tricked my superiors by telling them that it was the anniversary of my father's death and I succeeded in obtaining the leave. Since it was winter and I belonged to the ski regiment, I took my army skis and uniform with me. There was a hill in Kozowa between the pharmacy and the bathhouse and I skied down it. The snow was deep and the people of Kozowa had never seen skis and didn't know that one could travel on two long boards. When they saw me, they talked about how Josio Beker was wearing a Polish uniform and was skiing and had no fear at all.

Since I was a good soldier and always tidy, I was able to ask my superior for another leave. The base was only thirty-six kilometres from my town, so I went home every Wednesday and Thursday, travelling on my skis from the regiment. At Christmas, the sergeant called me in and informed me that I was to keep an eye on a certain town and take army horses with me in case there was any disorder during the holiday. He told me to choose twelve Jews to groom and clean the horses every day. I took Hershele with me. He was frightened of horses, so I chose a very gentle horse for him but as the horse galloped he screamed, crying that his behind hurt. I stopped the horse and took him off. I still laugh when I remember it.

Once, we were learning how to shoot with bullets. When it was my turn, I thought I had shot well, but it turned out I hadn't hit the target. I was punished for this. Instead of sitting at the table with everyone, I had to serve the soup. This took me so long that my food got cold, but I was so hungry that I ate it even though it tasted terrible.

When I went to the well to wash my canteen, two soldiers standing there called me a *parszywy zyd*, a lousy Jew. I was so angry that without giving it too much thought, I hit one of them with my canteen, splitting his skull. The next day, I was asked to report and given three days in the slammer. This meant I had to sleep on a hard bench and receive only half a loaf of bread and water. I slept there one night. In the morning the sergeant came to take me out because a general had arrived and they wanted me to present him with gifts at Piłsudski's monument. Despite the fact that I was a "dirty Jew," I was still the best soldier in the whole company. How I cursed them!

Although three months earlier I had been on leave, I was not embarrassed at all about going to the captain again to ask for more time off. I told him that every three months I had to observe the anniversary of my father's death, as that was the Jewish custom, which was not at all true. He consented, and at the same time Hershele also got a leave, so we two soldiers arrived in Kozowa for a break.

Hershele belonged to a Zionist youth organization called Betar, while I belonged to the Histadrut, a different Zionist organization. While we were home, however, Betar had an event one evening and Hershele invited me to attend. The girls made a big deal about us both being soldiers. I met a girl named Jenny Shleiber and spent the night dancing with her. Our days off sped by, and before long, Hershele and I returned to the army.

After eighteen months, I was discharged and became a civilian. I have to admit that serving in the Polish army made a man out of me, which was not a bad thing. The day I got my civilian clothes back and threw off my Polish uniform, I went back to my home town. My mother, my brothers, my little sister and I celebrated. Two days later, I went back to work, back to wheeling and dealing.

∿

In 1939, the war broke out between Germany and Poland. As a soldier in the Polish army, I was mobilized and had to leave immediately for

Rzeszów to join the Pilík Podhalańska, a regiment from the Podhale region that took its name after a kind of bird. The soldiers wore a feather in their caps. We drove all night and in the morning we were taken to a school and given military uniforms, including boots, trousers and a jacket. The Poles didn't have any more hats, so they requisitioned a factory that made berets. I was given a beret and, once again, looked like an officer. I was also lucky to have received a rifle because only one in twenty-five soldiers got one, although we weren't given any bullets. There I was, a Polish soldier with a beret on my head and a rifle without bullets, on my way to fight the Germans.

The Germans had begun bombing us. We were in retreat and they were in pursuit. I didn't have the strength to run, but I saw civilians running away, and I saw many students fleeing on bicycles. I thought to myself, I could escape faster on a bicycle. With my rifle-without-bullets, I went out to the road, stopped a couple of students and told them I was confiscating their bicycle because I was a soldier and had to retreat from the Germans. They stood in front of me, refusing to hand over their bicycle. Without any hesitation, I took the rifle off my shoulder and said, "In the name of the Polish Republic, I am confiscating your bicycle." They were terrified, not knowing, of course, that the rifle had no bullets, and they handed it over. I left them and beat a retreat. The Germans pursued us, bombing the main roads, their airplanes flying low in order to shoot at Polish soldiers. I saw soldiers dropping like flies.

On one occasion, an airplane flew over us with a Polish eagle painted on it. The Polish soldiers were relieved to see a Polish aircraft. It was flying low so the soldiers waved their handkerchiefs. All at once, there was machine gun fire, and about fifty Polish soldiers were gunned down. A German airplane had managed to trick us. Without looking back, I continued riding the bicycle – until one of the wheels broke off. I threw it into a ditch and found another student from whom I could take another bicycle. That was really the way it was.

Even with the new bicycle I had acquired, it soon became impossible to drive on the roads. I had to ride through fields because of the bombing. I rode on until I came to a trench of Polish soldiers. The captain stopped me, took away my rifle and the bicycle, and told me to get into the trench with the other soldiers to try to stop the Germans. We lay in the trench the entire night and the whole next day, not knowing what to do. A second night approached and passed and, early the next morning, the Germans began shooting. Bullets were landing right beside me. One soldier had already lost his head. The captain was shouting for us to leave the trench in single file. I got up immediately and could see German tanks in the distance. As the captain got on a motorcycle in an attempt to escape, I impulsively jumped into the sidecar. He looked like he wanted to kill me, but he was mid-escape and had no choice but to take me with him.

When we arrived at headquarters, I was given a pass to go to Romania. My plan, however, was to go to Romania via Kozowa. In the first village I came to, I asked where the head of the village lived. I ordered him to provide me with a horse and wagon and a good driver because I had to report to the Romanian border. Before long, I was given what I'd asked for, got into the wagon and told the driver to go to Czernowitz so that I could drive through my home town. It was a Friday evening that I drove into Kozowa with that horse and wagon. When I knocked on our window, my mother was overjoyed. I told the driver to go back while I stayed in my house and went to sleep.

Saturday morning the whole town came running and began asking if I had seen any of their boys in the army. Everyone wanted to know how the Poles were fighting the war. It did not take long before two policemen came to arrest me for desertion. I showed them my pass but, nonetheless, they told me that I had to leave Kozowa. I said goodbye to my family. Along with three other Polish soldiers, a horse and a wagon, we were on our way to Czernowitz.

After we had driven for about fifty kilometres, one of the soldiers suggested that perhaps we should run away. I would have agreed, but another soldier took out his revolver and said that whoever wanted

to run away would be shot. I was afraid. I waited for the right opportunity and, when the soldier with the revolver wasn't looking, I told
that first one that he had been right. We should run away. He believed
me, and I became his friend, but I sensed that I should not travel with
them much longer. At one point, I told the others that I had to relieve
myself and was going into the woods. I said I wouldn't take long and
that they should drive slowly and I would catch up. They let me go.
But I went into the woods and didn't return. That's how I escaped
from the Polish army.

I wandered around in the woods before coming to a road. I followed the fields alongside the road, eventually approaching a village.
Then, some Ukrainians caught me and forced me to take off my army
clothes, which were new. They even took my trousers, leaving me
only in my underwear. I was lucky, however, because I knew one of
the men. Before the war, he had been a buyer for a Ukrainian cooperative and therefore he let me go free. I made my way back to
Kozowa, only to find that the Soviets were already in our town. And
now, new troubles began.

The Soviets and the Germans

I remember it as though it were today. The Soviets came into Kozowa and told us that they had come to save us. People believed them. What do people from a small town like Kozowa know? The Soviets said that Poland had asked for their help. But the Soviet thieves helped themselves first. One of their commanders got up on an iron barrel in the centre of the marketplace and made a speech, saying, "We have factories! We have oranges! We have food!" At least some in the crowd were convinced that the Soviets were tricking us and really had nothing to offer us at all.

To begin with, the Soviets took the keys away from all the shopkeepers. If someone had a small business from which he barely made a living, it too was confiscated. One of the first things they did was take one of my mother's cows. We only had three cows, which helped my mother earn a living and allowed her to have milk for the children. I remember my mother shouting at them, "Are you done yet?" It wasn't long before they took a second cow. They didn't allow anyone to have three cows because whoever had three cows was not considered "one of them" – a worker. That is how they destroyed the businesses.

The Soviets created a local police force and a secret police force, the NKVD. The local police force was comprised of poor Jewish boys and poor non-Jews, all communists who, under the Poles, had been put in jail prior to May Day to prevent them from organizing a parade. They were later released. Among those boys were a few friends of mine. The tailor, Wolf Reichenberg, who had previously been detained as a communist, was now appointed head of the town. Although he was a poor tailor, he was well-educated. He had been the leader of the Histadrut Zionist movement, to which I also belonged.

The Soviets issued passports, and since I had grown up an orphan, without a father, they wrote in my passport that I was a *bednyak*, a poor man. That meant that I was one of them – no one could accuse me of being bourgeois. I got a driving permit from the Soviets and became a chauffeur for the director of the Land Department. I was given an Italian car, a Fiat 508, and every Sunday I had to drive my boss around to the villages. He would wait for the peasants to get out of church and then stand on an iron barrel and lecture everyone on the merits of becoming a *kolkhoznik* a member of a collective farm. He tried to convince them that life would be very good if they gave up their land. The poor peasants agreed because they had nothing to lose, but the wealthier peasants weren't too happy.

After a speech, we went to the local tavern to eat dumplings, called *vareniki*. My boss always began drinking before the meal and soon he no longer knew what he was doing. He insisted that I drink along with him, not from a small glass but from a tea glass, which was more than I could drink. When he put his glass of whisky to his mouth, I spilled mine under the table.

Since I had a good job, everyone was envious of me, especially because I drove a car. In our town we saw pigs roaming the streets, not cars. The children ran after me when I drove home, and my mother was proud. I remember starting that Fiat 508 with a hand crank. When I had to go downhill, I turned off the gas. I had to fix everything myself.

And so I drove with my Soviet boss each Sunday to a different village, where he would get out at the church and stand on a barrel to tell the villagers to create a *kolkhoz*, like they had in the Soviet Union.

One time, after one such speech, the head of the village invited him to eat and drink. For the Soviets, however, a chauffeur is an important person and the boss didn't want to eat without me. He said to me, "Chauffeur, we are going to have something to eat." Did I have a choice? I drove over to the house with him. On the table were two litres of whisky and long sausages. They drank a toast with tea glasses, and soon one bottle was completely empty. I turned around and saw the hostess bringing a pot of dumplings, and then the feast began. The boss was soon drunk. Yet again, I tricked him – when he said, "Na zdorovye!" (To your health!) and put his glass of whiskey to his lips, I spilled mine under the table. That's what we did every Sunday. All in all, I didn't have it so bad.

Week after week I drove around like this, until October, the holiday of Simchas Torah. The Soviets didn't like celebrations of any Jewish holidays, but in a town like Kozowa, all the holidays were celebrated. On a joyous holiday like Simchas Torah, a festival that celebrates the Torah being given to the Jews, I didn't want to drive around with my boss. I thought he was crazy for wanting me to drive him to the villages on a holiday such as this. We didn't have telephones so he sent the secretary, whose name was Beyle Schechter, to come get me. She said that the boss had ordered me to drive him on that day. I replied that if he lived to see that happen, he would live to see the Messiah. On a holy day like Simchas Torah, I wouldn't drive. She reported back everything I had said. My boss was angry, but I didn't budge. I disobeyed him and kept the holiday.

All my friends got together and we each chipped in a few złotys to buy a small keg of beer to drink for Simchas Torah. Meanwhile, my boss, who didn't have a driving permit, took the car himself and ended up driving it into a ditch. He took me to court for disobeying his order, for which I could have been sentenced to five years. I stood before the Soviet prosecutor at the courthouse shaking with fear. I had brought character witnesses with me: a woman and two more non-Jews from the marketplace. Believe me, I was terrified. The only thing that saved me was the *bednyak* designation on my passport.

Although I was freed, from that time on I was still afraid of what could happen. Even though Reichenberg, the man in charge of the town, knew me, for the time being, I didn't drive the car anymore. Eight days later, I received another summons to appear at the court. Shaking, I ran to speak to the Soviet prosecutor, whom I knew well because I had brought him two pairs of shoes from Lwów for his children. I told him the whole story about Simchas Torah, about how it was an important holiday for us. I also told him that the springs in the car were broken and that, therefore, I was in the right because according to the law it was illegal to drive with broken springs. He told me in Russian, "We'll see."

When I went to make my case in court, I could see that this was going to be a real trial. In the courtroom sat the two character witnesses from our town, a woman who sold apples and the tailor Reichenberg. I knew all of them, so I felt more at ease. They would protect me. It was decided that my boss didn't have the right to drive the car without a permit, and they set me free again.

The next day when I came to work, my boss didn't want to speak to me, but he had no choice. He sat with me in the car and, taking out his revolver, said, "What do you think? The Soviets are in charge here. I'll have you put in jail." Without thinking, I told him in Russian, "Go shoot yourself!" and I got out of the car.

After that, I began buying pigs, calves, flax and grain in Kozowa and selling them in Lwów. I got to know the Kozowa procurator and I began to make big business deals. Of course, dealing in the black market under the Soviets was punishable by death. I was successful once, twice, but I saw that I could end up in jail, and who would get me out this time? I decided that I would only buy and sell meat. I asked my friend Reichenberg to give me a permit to drive to Lwów. I was allowed to travel to Lwów because, as I mentioned, I was a *bednyak*.

I bought some pigs in Kozowa, which were cleaned and put into sacks for me to take to the train station. I had bribed the manager of that small station. My brother Srul Hersh harnessed my horse and was supposed to drive me to the station and take the horse home. Srul Hersh worked as the manager of a pastry shop. We drove out at midnight, but on the way the NKVD caught up with us. They didn't know me, but they knew my brother and couldn't believe that he was a speculator. They found the six bags of pork and ordered me to turn my wagon around and drive to the police. I drove in the dark, with them following. It occurred to me that I should stop the NKVD and say that I didn't know where I was supposed to go. At that point, I told my brother to throw two sacks of meat into the ditch, but he was too afraid. I threw one sack into the ditch.

When we arrived at the NKVD headquarters in Kozowa, they unloaded the sacks of meat and found one missing. One of the NKVD men drove back and returned with the sack. I was sure that five years in prison were awaiting me. I told the NKVD officer that I had an agreement with a family in Lwów that I would eat and sleep at their place for six months but I had to give them a lot of meat in exchange. I also told him that I had a permit from the head of the town, Reichenberg. This worked and they let me go. Reichenberg warned me that he couldn't do me any more favours like that, and so I stopped doing business.

In June 1941, many young men from our town, including me, had to go by foot from Kozowa to Tarnopol, where we were to be inducted into the Soviet army. Seeing my mother's tears was terrible but, having already been a soldier in the Polish army, being drafted again had no impact on me. Anyone who had one hand or one foot was good enough for the Soviets. What else could they do? There was a war going on, with the Germans right behind us. Everywhere, people were running away.

By the end of June, bombs were falling on Tarnopol and Lwów. The Soviets kept retreating, and my platoon with them. In Tarnopol, German airplanes followed us from the air, dropping bombs. I saw soldiers killed before my eyes. I was right beside them, but I think that because I believed in God, the bombs and bullets missed me. When the bombing stopped, we continued on our way. I had a pair of new boots, a uniform, and a belt for carrying bullets, but I hadn't been given any ammunition, or a gun for that matter. They also had no hats to give us. We were led like a flock of sheep, every seven soldiers accompanied by an NKVD man with a revolver in his hand because the government didn't trust anyone from the western Ukraine. We were forced to walk for fifty kilometres without any food.

Taking advantage of an opportunity when our NKVD guard was not watching us too closely, I, along with the other six soldiers who were with me, ran into a forest. We didn't know where we were. First we rested. My feet were very tired and the skin was blistered and chafed. We waited for dark to decide what to do. At night we heard shooting, but we didn't move. Then, we waited for daylight, got up and left the forest.

We soon saw three Soviet officers, who also saw us and shouted for us to stop. They came over to us, carrying rifles. I was trembling. They swore at us, "You Zapadniki [westerners], f**k you!" They guessed that we were deserters and took us up a hill to shoot us. After lining us up to be executed, one of them asked us our nationality. The six non-Jews said that they were Ukrainians. When he asked me, I said I was a Jew. On hearing that, for some reason he ordered the two others to hold their fire, and he put me in charge of taking the Ukrainians to Zhitomir to deliver them to their unit. I told him that I was younger than the Ukrainians and asked him to make one of the older ones the commander. He swore so loudly that I thought I would die. He pointed me in the right direction, and I took charge of the six Ukrainians.

After we had walked ten kilometres through fields without seeing another soldier, the Ukrainians said that they would go no further. I sat with them in the field and we deliberated what to do next. We decided to go to the nearest village. On the way we saw a gaggle of geese from a Russian *kolkhoz*. We ran after the geese until we cornered one. One of the Ukrainians grabbed it by the feet and twisted its head off. We were very hungry. We took the goose, plucked its feathers and cut it into pieces. But we still needed to cook it. When I recall all this, it horrifies me. Back then, I felt like only a non-Jew could do what that Ukrainian had, and I worried that for them, a goose and a Jew were the same. I always had a hard time trusting non-Jews.

We went to the road, saw a peasant and asked him whether the Soviet army was in the nearby village. He said that the Soviets were no longer anywhere to be seen, only Germans, and that we were surrounded and could go no further. We then approached a little house in a field. An old peasant woman there also told us that the Germans were already in the village, but that she would let us cook the goose. The woman lit the stove and put the goose and a few potatoes into a large iron pot. We waited for the goose to cook, but it was an old goose and did not become soft. We had no choice, though, so we ate tough goose and potato soup.

What could we do now that we were surrounded by Germans? There was no escape. I had the idea of taking a white towel and giving ourselves up. Leaving the house, we immediately saw German soldiers. We held up the white towel and they ordered us all to put up our hands. They searched us and told us to sit in the field. There were already about five hundred captured Soviets sitting there. A large truck filled with cartons of eggs was there too, and everyone was given six raw eggs. The Germans had taken these eggs but didn't know what to do with so many of them so they gave them to their captives. We made a fire, and everyone roasted his six eggs and ate them. The Soviet soldiers remarked that it was better to be captured by the Germans than by the Soviet army, which never gave out any food.

We sat in the field until dusk. Just before nightfall, large trucks arrived. We were told to climb on the trucks and were driven to a small town called Starokonstantinov. There, we were ordered to get off the trucks and again sit in a field because there was a large hole in the road, which had been recently bombed by the Soviets. Then I saw with my own eyes how the Germans took about one hundred Jews, beat them and forced them to dismantle their houses and use the bricks and rocks to fill in the hole. Only then did I understand that I must not say I was a Jew. I went over to the six Ukrainians and asked them not to tell anyone that I was Jewish. I had a silver wristwatch and I wanted to give it to one of the Ukrainians in exchange for the cross he was wearing, but he assured me that no one would reveal that I was Jewish. And, indeed, that is what happened. Before then, I would not have believed that six Ukrainians would protect me and not turn me in.

We were led away to a large building in some sort of an army camp. The Soviets had stored grain there but it was now completely empty. Approximately five thousand captured Soviets were packed into the building. There were also Uzbeks, Ukrainians, Poles and, of course, Jews. The Germans were especially interested in finding the Jews. At first, the Germans asked the prisoners of various nationalities whether any of them could speak or understand German to help them translate. Many of the prisoners called out that they either understood or spoke it.

We were locked up in the building, without food. After two days, people became like wild animals. We had to relieve ourselves where we were, one lying beside the other. It stank so much that I could not bear it any longer; I decided that I had to escape. I had noticed that each morning at 8:00 a.m. the Germans opened the door. They would only ask if there were any Jews and, without fail, the Poles and the Ukrainians would point a few out. The Jews were then beaten so badly that blood flowed.

One time, someone pointed out a Jew to the Germans, who then proceeded to severely beat this man. This time, however, there were non-Jews who were very annoyed about this. The next morning, when the Germans opened the gate and asked who was a Jew, these non-Jews pointed out the man who had given up the Jew the previous day. The Germans beat this non-Jew mercilessly. He shrieked, but they kept on beating him. They killed him like a pig. I will never forget this.

I worried about how I could avoid the same fate from such German bandits, especially when I was a Jew. I started to feel anxious about trusting my six Ukrainian companions. All I could think of was escaping. Still, they didn't give me away. I do not know, to this day, why they did not hand me over to the Germans. For this reason, I have to believe that there is a God.

Every morning, when they opened the door, the German soldiers used their bayonets to make space for themselves by stabbing prisoners who were in their way. I couldn't stand it any longer and was resigned to being shot. Then, it occurred to me to pretend that I was wounded in one leg. I took off my boot, bandaged my foot and went to the door. The next morning, I asked one of the German soldiers to let me go to the well, which was not far from the building, so I could fill my canteen with water. He let me go. I filled the canteen and drank as much as I could, and then I filled it again to bring back to my Ukrainian friends. When I got back to the building, the poor captured soldiers wanted that water so desperately that they all tried to grab it and the water spilled on the ground.

It was now three weeks since we had been given any food. Everyone was lying on the floor looking for seeds under the boards. I could no longer stand on my feet. Again, my Ukrainian companions came to my aid. They had somehow stolen a few pieces of sugar and woke me up to give me some, which kept me alive. It really did. All the captured Soviet soldiers lay one next to the other, many wounded. How could anyone survive such conditions?

I continued to look for a way out. I told my friends that the next day I would again stand at the door and ask for water and then try to escape. I told one, Ivan, that he should take my coat and rucksack if I was successful. I had made up my mind to escape, even if I risked getting shot. I got up around 7:00 a.m. and, with my bandaged foot, I went to stand at the door. I heard the door open and the Germans asking again for Jews. There were Jews who had not yet been handed over – they were pointed out and beaten. I was still afraid that perhaps my Ukrainian friends would change their minds and point me out, if not today then the next day. Again I showed a German soldier that I wanted to fetch a drink. He looked at my bandaged foot and let me go to get water. But my goal was not water, but escape.

On my way to the well, I had a good look around. I saw an army kitchen where captured Soviets were chopping wood. I went over to them and began chopping wood also. I hoped the Germans guarding the kitchen would look away for five minutes. Then I noticed a passageway between two buildings. There were prisoners housed in the two buildings, with only a narrow passageway between them. I thought that if I could get into that passageway, I could escape to the other side at night. I stayed around the kitchen until dusk, when the German soldier told us to go back into the building. When the German's back was turned, I hid between the two buildings. He hadn't seen me, and I stayed there until dark.

At night, the Germans locked the gate to the building where the prisoners were held. Lying in the passageway, without moving, I heard everything going on. The guards did not leave. Some of them paced back and forth, watching over the place. I still thought that I could get out through the passage between the buildings and make it to the other side. I crawled for about one hundred metres and then stuck my head out of the passageway to check the other side of the building. There too, I saw guards walking back and forth. I hid and waited for them to leave so I could make my escape. I felt trapped and saw death before me, but I did not give in to despair.

I could see that it was hard to escape, but what was I to do? I thought that I should crawl back and see whether I could get back to the building where I had been held for the past few weeks. But how could I get into the building if it was locked and the Germans were guarding it? I risked my life. When the German turned around and marched in the other direction, I came out and shouted, "Halt!" The German was startled, not knowing where the shout was coming from. I told him that I had been working in the kitchen and got locked out. He unlocked the door to the building and let me in. I found my Ukrainian companions and told them what had happened to me. Then I lay down and fell asleep from exhaustion.

In the morning, it seemed like a lot of noise and action was going on. The door was opened earlier than usual, and the German soldiers ordered that henceforth Ukrainians should be kept separate from everyone else. I went with my Ukrainian friends as a Ukrainian, shaking, not fully trusting the situation. Nevertheless, I stayed with them. I knew how to speak Ukrainian very well and I did not look like a Jew, which helped me a lot. Everyone was given a loaf of bread, and the German soldiers let us out. Imagine five thousand prisoners being led away. Where we were going, no one knew.

~

EDITOR'S NOTE

Joseph Beker passed away before completing his memoir. His daughter Marilyn was able to fill in some of the information missing from his account.

After Joseph was taken away with the other Ukrainian prisoners-of-war, they marched for days, guarded by the Nazis, along roads with fields on either side. Finally, exhausted and tired of it all, Joseph decided to make a run for it no matter what happened. He once again used the old "toilet trick" and stepped into a field. He lowered his trousers and squatted, and then when the guards weren't looking, he ran for it. Someone noticed him and began to shoot. The bullets flew but, magically, they all missed him. He kept running. Perhaps he was out of range, or perhaps the Nazis decided not to chase him because they were concerned about losing control of the other prisoners. Either way, his bravery paid off. He hid during the days and travelled at night, eventually making his way back home to Kozowa.

In Kozowa, for a short period of time, Joseph was able to pass for a gentile. Well-dressed in high riding boots, jodhpurs and a jacket, the Nazis seemed to take no notice of him. When a family he knew was scheduled to be deported, he raised the money to "buy" them back from the Nazis. Joseph went to the commandant's office with a large amount of cash, and the commandant took the money and released the family, but not before he and the other officers beat Joseph to a pulp. They kicked him out and shouted, "Hey, you're dressed like a lord, you better go to America!" Joseph continued to help other families avoid deportation for as long as he could.

In September 1942, the Nazis rounded up 1,000 Jews and deported them to the Belzec death camp; the raids and roundups continued throughout the year. Joseph, like Bronia, hid from each roundup with his family. In April 1943, when Bronia's family died in the bunker, he gave her shelter and took care of her. His mandate to never give up helped them both survive the war.

Glossary

Ander's Army The informal name for the Polish Armed Forces in the East that was led by General Władysław Anders (1892–1970) between 1941 and 1946. In June 1941, after Germany invaded the Soviet Union, Anders, who had been a POW since 1939, was released by the Soviets to establish an armed force of exiled Poles living in the USSR to assist the Red Army in its fight against Germany. By 1942 this force, known as Ander's Army, included approximately 72,000 combatants – among them between 4,000 and 5,000 Jews.

banderowcy (Ukrainian) The informal term for Ukrainian nationalist guerillas led by Stepan Bandera under the auspices of the Organization of Ukrainian Nationalists (OUN) and its military wing, the Ukrainska Povstanska Armiya (UPA). Many of its members were antisemitic and led anti-Jewish pogroms after the war. The UPA was formally disbanded in 1949 but continued to have a localized presence until 1956.

bednyak (Russian) One of three categories of peasants under the Soviet communist class system. *Bednyaks* were poor peasants; *serednyaks*, mid-income peasants; and *kulaks*, higher-income farmers who, having larger farms than most Russian peasants, were considered "class enemies."

Betar A Zionist youth movement founded by Revisionist Zionist leader Ze'ev Jabotinsky in 1923 that encouraged the develop-
ment of a new generation of Zionist activists based on the ideals
of courage, self-respect, military training, defence of Jewish life
and property, and settlement in Israel to establish a Jewish state in
British Mandate Palestine. In 1934, Betar membership in Poland
numbered more than 40,000. During the 1930s and 1940s, as antisemitism increased and the Nazis launched their murderous
campaign against the Jews of Europe, Betar rescued thousands
of Jews by organizing illegal immigration to British Mandate Palestine. The Betar movement today, closely aligned with Israel's
right-wing Likud party, remains involved in supporting Jewish
and Zionist activism around the world.

beys midrash (Yiddish; house of learning) A Jewish religious study
centre.

British Mandate Palestine The area of the Middle East under British
rule from 1923 to 1948, as established by the League of Nations
after World War I. During that time, the United Kingdom severely
restricted Jewish immigration. The Mandate area encompassed
present-day Israel, Jordan, the West Bank and the Gaza Strip.

cheder (Hebrew; literally, room) An Orthodox Jewish elementary
school that teaches the fundamentals of Jewish religious observance and textual study, as well as the Hebrew language.

cholent (Yiddish) A traditional Jewish slow-cooked pot stew usually
eaten as the main course at the festive Shabbat lunch on Saturdays
after the synagogue service and on other Jewish holidays. For Jews
of Eastern-European descent, the basic ingredients of *cholent* are
meat, potatoes, beans and barley.

chremzlach (Yiddish) Pancakes made from matzah meal, eaten during the Passover holiday. *See also* matzo; Passover.

golem (Hebrew; in Yiddish, goylem) In Jewish folklore, a man made
of clay brought to life by a rabbi or mystic. One of the golem's leg-
endary characteristics was that it doesn't speak, so calling some-

one a "goylem" was a derogatory expression for someone who was helpless, dumb or mute.

Hasidic Judaism (from the Hebrew word *hasid*; literally, piety) An Orthodox Jewish spiritual movement founded by Rabbi Israel ben Eliezer in eighteenth-century Poland; characterized by philosophies of mysticism and a focus on joyful prayer. This movement resulted in a new kind of leader who attracted disciples as opposed to the traditional rabbis who focused on the intellectual study of Jewish law. Melody and dance have an important role in Hasidic worship. There are many different sects of Hasidic Judaism, but followers of Hasidism often wear dark, conservative clothes as well as a head covering to reflect modesty and show respect to God.

havdala (Hebrew; separation) A ceremony that marks the end of the Sabbath. During *havdala*, blessings are recited over a braided candle, lit to symbolize the light of Shabbat, a kiddush cup of wine, symbolizing joy, and a spice box to symbolize the sweetness of the Sabbath *See also* kiddush; Shabbat.

Histadrut (Hebrew; abbreviation of HaHistadrut HaKlalit shel Ha-Ovdim B'Eretz Yisrael; in English, General Federation of Labourers in the Land of Israel) A labour union established in pre-state Israel in 1920 that was also a Zionist organization, with similar socialist ideals, in pre-war Poland. *See also* Zionism.

Judenrat (German; pl. *Judenräte*) Jewish Council. A group of Jewish leaders appointed by the Germans to administer and provide services to the local Jewish population under occupation and carry out German orders. The *Judenräte*, which appeared to be self-governing entities but were actually under complete German control, faced difficult and complex moral decisions under brutal conditions and remain a contentious subject. The chairmen had to decide whether to comply or refuse to comply with German demands. Some were killed by the Nazis for refusing, while others committed suicide. Jewish officials who advocated compliance thought that cooperation might save at least some Jews. Some who denounced resistance efforts did so because they believed that armed resistance would bring death to the entire community.

Kaddish (Aramaic; holy) Also known as the Mourner's Prayer, Kaddish is said as part of mourning rituals in Jewish prayer services as well as at funerals and memorials.

kiddush (Hebrew; literally, sanctification) The blessing over wine that is recited on Shabbat and other Jewish holidays. *See also* Shabbat.

kolkhoz (Russian; abbreviation of *kollektivnoe khozyaistvo*; collective farm) A cooperative agricultural enterprise that operated on state-owned land in the USSR. The *kolkhoz* was the dominant form of agricultural enterprise in the former Soviet Union.

kosher (Hebrew) Fit to eat according to Jewish dietary laws. Observant Jews follow a system of rules known as *kashruth* that regulates what can be eaten, how food is prepared and how meat and poultry are slaughtered. Food is kosher when it has been deemed fit for consumption according to this system of rules. There are several foods that are forbidden, most notably pork products and shellfish. *See also* shoychet.

kulich (Russian) A tall, cylindrical bread traditionally eaten around Easter in Eastern European countries.

Maariv (Hebrew) The evening Jewish prayer service.

matzo (Hebrew; also matza, matzoh, matsah; in Yiddish, matze) Crisp flatbread, made of plain white flour and water, that is not allowed to rise before or during baking. Matzo is the substitute for bread during the Jewish holiday of Passover, when eating bread and leavened products is forbidden. *See also* Passover.

May Day Also known as International Workers' Day, May Day is celebrated on May 1 in many countries around the world in recognition of the achievements of workers and the international labour movement. It was first celebrated in Russia on May 1, 1917. In countries other than Canada and the United States – where Labour Day is considered the official holiday for workers – May

Day is marked by huge street rallies led by workers, trade unions, anarchists and various communist and socialist parties.

mensch (Yiddish) A good, decent person, with honourable qualities; mensch generally refers to someone who is selfless or who has integrity.

mikveh (Hebrew; literally, a pool or gathering of water) A ritual purification bath taken by Jews on occasions that denote change, such as before the Sabbath (signifying the shift from a regular weekday to a holy day of rest), as well as those that denote a change in personal status, such as before a person's wedding or, for a married woman, after menstruation. The word mikveh refers to both the pool of water and the building that houses the ritual bath.

Mincha (Hebrew) The afternoon Jewish prayer service. *See also* Maariv.

moyre-hoyro'es A term coined from the Hebrew phrase *moreh hora'ah*, meaning "one who teaches instruction." *Moreh hora'ah*, a generic term referring to an expert in Jewish law, is a standard way to refer to a rabbi or a judge in religious matters.

NKVD (Russian) The acronym of the Narodnyi Komissariat Vnutrennikh Del, meaning People's Commissariat for Internal Affairs. The NKVD functioned as the Soviet Union's security agency, secret police and intelligence agency from 1934 to 1954. The NKVD's Main Directorate for State Security (GUGB) was the forerunner of the Committee for State Security, better known as the KGB (acronym for Komitet Gosudarstvennoy Bezopasnosti) established in 1954. The organization's stated dual purpose was to defend the USSR from external dangers from foreign powers and to protect the Communist Party from perceived dangers within. Under Stalin, the pursuit of imagined conspiracies against the state became a central focus and the NKVD played a critical role in suppressing political dissent.

Orthodox Judaism The set of beliefs and practices of Jews for whom the observance of Jewish law is closely connected to faith; it is characterized by strict religious observance of Jewish dietary laws, restrictions on work on the Sabbath and holidays, and a code of modesty in dress.

Passover One of the major festivals of the Jewish calendar, Passover takes place over eight days in the spring. One of the main observances of the holiday is to recount the story of Exodus, the Jews' flight from slavery in Egypt, at a ritual meal called a seder. The name itself refers to the fact that God "passed over" the houses of the Jews when he set about slaying the firstborn sons of Egypt as the last of the ten plagues aimed at convincing Pharaoh to free the Jews.

Piłsudski, Józef (1867–1935) Leader of the Second Polish Republic from 1926 to 1935. Piłsudski was largely responsible for achieving Poland's independence in 1918 after more than a century of being partitioned by Russia, Austria and Prussia. Piłsudski's regime was notable for improving the lot of ethnic minorities, including Poland's large Jewish population. He followed a policy of "state-assimilation" whereby citizens were judged not by their ethnicity but by their loyalty to the state. Many Polish Jews felt that his regime was key to keeping the antisemitic currents in Poland in check. When Piłsudski died in 1935, the quality of life of Poland's Jews deteriorated once again.

rebbe (Yiddish; teacher) The spiritual leader or teacher of a Hasidic movement.

Shabbat (Hebrew; in Yiddish, Shabbes, Shabbos) The weekly day of rest beginning Friday at sunset and ending Saturday at sundown, ushered in by the lighting of candles on Friday night and the recitation of blessings over wine and challah (egg bread); a day of celebration as well as prayer, it is customary to eat three festive meals, attend synagogue services and refrain from doing any work or travelling.

shalosh seudos (Yiddish; third meal) The smallest of three meals eaten on Shabbat. Typical practice was to have two meals a day, so having three meals on the Sabbath signified the honour of the day.

shegetz A non-Jewish male. The Hebrew origin of the word is "sheketz," meaning "impurity." Modern usage of the term can be either humorous or derogatory, depending on the context.

sheytl (Yiddish; wig) A head covering worn by Orthodox Jewish women to abide by religious codes of modesty. *See also* Orthodox.

shiksa A non-Jewish female. *See also* shegetz.

shoychet (Yiddish; ritual slaughterer) A learned man conversant with the religious teaching of *kashruth*, the system of rules in Jewish tradition, trained to slaughter animals painlessly and to check that the product meets the various criteria of kosher slaughter. *See also* kosher.

shtetl (Yiddish) Small town. A small village or town with a predominantly Jewish population that existed before World War II in Central and Eastern Europe, where life revolved around Judaism and Judaic culture. In the Middle Ages, Jews were not allowed to own land, so the shtetl developed as a refuge for Jews.

shtreimel A fur-rimmed hat worn by Hasidic Jews on the Sabbath and other major Jewish holidays.

Simchas Torah (Hebrew; literally, rejoicing in the Torah) The holiday that marks the conclusion of the annual cycle of readings from the Torah and the beginning of a new cycle. The holiday is celebrated in synagogue by singing and dancing with the Torah scrolls.

speculator (in Russian, *spekulant*) The Soviet term for someone selling something for profit. In the USSR, free market activity was considered anathema to both communist ideology and the centrally planned, state-controlled economy that was the cornerstone of the Soviet system. The intent to resell anything for profit – speculating – was a very serious crime. A speculator was considered to be a "parasite," working in opposition to the "socially useful labour" that was the duty of every Soviet citizen, and was therefore seen as an enemy of the state.

Strettener The Hasidic dynasty of Rabbi Yehuda Hirsch Brandwein of Stratyn, Galicia, now in the Western Ukraine.

tchines (Yiddish; prayers) Seventeenth-century Yiddish prayer books created by and written for women. As most prayer books were written in Hebrew, solely for male worshippers, *tchines* represented a significant turning point in women's religious lives and participation.

treyf (Yiddish) Food that is not allowed under Jewish dietary laws. *See also* kosher.

Tsena u'Rena (Yiddish; Come Out and See) The first major original work to be written in Yiddish for women. In the early 1600s, it was a collection of traditional biblical commentary and folklore tied to the weekly Torah readings.

Yiddish A language derived from Middle High German with elements of Hebrew, Aramaic, Romance and Slavic languages, and written in Hebrew characters. Spoken by Jews in east-central Europe for roughly a thousand years from the tenth century to the mid-twentieth century, it was still the most common language among European Jews until the outbreak of World War II. There are similarities between Yiddish and contemporary German.

Yom Kippur (Hebrew; literally, day of atonement) A solemn day of fasting and repentance that comes eight days after Rosh Hashanah, the Jewish New Year, and marks the end of the high holidays.

Zionism A movement promoted by the Viennese Jewish journalist Theodor Herzl, who argued in his 1896 book *Der Judenstaat* (The Jewish State) that the best way to resolve the problem of antisemitism and persecution of Jews in Europe was to create an independent Jewish state in the historic Jewish homeland of Biblical Israel. Zionists also promoted the revival of Hebrew as a Jewish national language. In interwar Poland, Zionism was one of many Jewish political parties with affiliated schools and youth groups.

Photographs

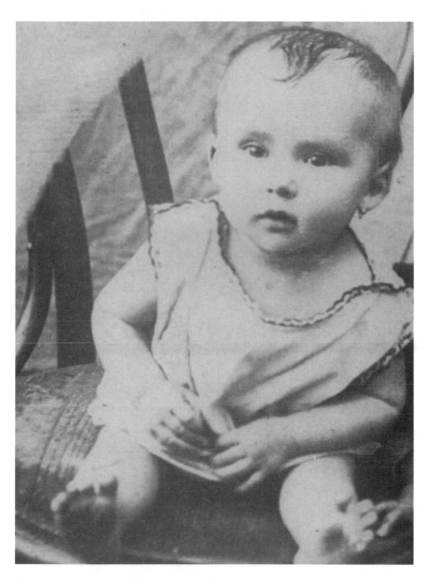

Bronia (née Rohatiner) Beker, age one. Kozowa, circa 1921.

Back row, left to right: Bronia's cousin Mechel, her sister, Sarah, and Bronia. Front row: Bronia's grandmother and her cousin Cyla. Kozowa, circa 1937.

1

2

1 The Rohatiner extended family before the war. Bronia (back row, fifth from the left) is standing beside her sister, Sarah. Their parents, Malka and Moses Rohatiner, are seated in the middle row. Kozowa, circa 1938.

2 Joseph Beker (standing, right) with his immediate family before the war. Left to right: Joseph's brother Shmuel, his sister, Esther, mother, Gitl, and brother Srul Hersh. Kozowa, circa 1927.

Bronia and Joseph Beker. Lodz, 1945.

1 Bronia and Joseph after the war with Elke Shütz, Bronia's maternal great-aunt.
2 The Bekers with their first daughter, Marilyn, great-aunt Elke, and cousin Cyla and her husband, Mechel. Austria, circa 1946.

1, 2, 3 & 4 Bronia and Joseph in the 1940s and 50s.

1

2

1 Bronia (far right) with her daughter Marilyn, her uncle Isaac Gold and his wife, Bayla, who sponsored the Beker family and helped them immigrate to Canada. Toronto, 1948.

2 Bronia, Marilyn, Joseph and baby Jeanne. Toronto, 1952.

Jeanne and Marilyn Beker, circa 1955.

1, 2 & 3 The Beker family in the 1950s and 60s.

1 & 2 Bronia and Joseph with their first granddaughter, Bekky. Toronto, 1987.
3 Jeanne's daughters, Bekky (right) and Joey. 1990.

Joseph and Bronia Beker, circa 1985.

Index

The Azrieli Foundation was established in 1989 to realize and extend the philanthropic vision of David J. Azrieli, C.M., C.Q., M.Arch. The Foundation's mission is to support a wide spectrum of initiatives in education and research. The Azrieli Foundation is an active supporter of programs in the fields of Education, the education of architects, scientific and medical research, and the arts. The Azrieli Foundation's many initiatives include: the Holocaust Survivor Memoirs Program, which collects, preserves, publishes and distributes the written memoirs of survivors in Canada; the Azrieli Institute for Educational Empowerment, an innovative program successfully working to keep at-risk youth in school; the Azrieli Fellows Program, which promotes academic excellence and leadership on the graduate level at Israeli universities; the Azrieli Music Project, which celebrates and fosters the creation of high-quality new Jewish orchestral music; and the Azrieli Neurodevelopmental Research Program, which supports advanced research on neurodevelopmental disorders, particularly Fragile X and Autism Spectrum Disorders.